The World According to Max

Real Lessons From
Real Business

Illustration – *Commercial Instruction* by Isidor Kaufmann, 1853 - 1921

WHAT OTHERS ARE SAYING . . .

"Part Aesop, part Jack Welch, Max Kupperman tells it like it really is. A wonderful job of presenting sage business advice in an easy-to-read narrative format. Whether you are a small business owner or a budding MBA, the stories in this book lay a solid foundation."

- Stephanie M., Colorado

"Kudos - business owners can read this and skip business and law school."

- Elizabeth W., California

"Very informative, could not put down. I felt like I was in the same room as the characters."

- Robert B., Arizona

"Wonderful, informative, inspiring at many levels. Deserves a wide audience."

- Janelle R., New Jersey

The World According to Max

Real Lessons From Real Business

Jim Redman

Copyright © 2013, 2016 by Jim Redman.

All rights reserved. Except as provided by U.S. and international copyright laws, no part of this publication may be reproduced, stored in a retrieval system or transmitted in any form or by any means without the prior written permission of the author, except for use of brief quotations in a review or journal.

This is a work of fiction. Names, characters, business establishments, places, events and incidents are either products of the author's imagination or used in a fictitious manner for literary effect. Any resemblance to actual persons, living or dead, or to actual events is purely coincidental.

Descriptions of legal, accounting and other principles are not to be taken as advice or guidance on these subjects. Readers are urged to seek competent professional help as appropriate in addressing their own circumstances and issues.

ISBN: 978-1535280198

DEDICATION

To those entrepreneurs and managers who have learned that success isn't final and that failure isn't fatal; and to the professionals who have helped them along the way.

CONTENTS

	Introduction	xi
1	For Richer Or Poorer	13
2	A Nice Friendly Banker	33
3	What A Great Place To Work	53
4	Live To Fight Another Day	71
5	Let's Make A Deal	87
6	Sunrise, Sunset	101
	The Author	109

Good judgment comes from experience, experience comes from bad judgment.

– Anon

INTRODUCTION

This is a story about real business, and especially the issues faced by real small business owners and their families.

I spent years building and running a good size company with many employees. Later, in my formal work on bankruptcy cases in Federal court, and as receiver and examiner in state court insolvency cases, I saw first hand the results of weak management, excessive spending and, especially, lack of planning. I've learned that most entrepreneurs get caught up with the upside potential of their ventures but are pretty naive about what it really takes to make it.

In my consulting practice, my associates and I have focused on working with ownership families to resolve serious problems. If they couldn't be resolved, we helped get them out so that they could live to fight another day. If a sale or merger was a possibility, we assisted in the negotiation and concluding of a transaction.

A word about the narrative. The central character, Max is a crusty curmudgeon who is brilliant but rather unforgiving. His assistant, Jay is a cocky millennial with sharp analytical skills. As a team they work very effectively on various client challenges. Although this is a work of fiction, every issue presented and resolved by Max and Jay is one actually encountered in my professional career.

Jim Redman
Wickenburg, Arizona

September 2016

email: jim@desertresources.com

1

For Richer Or Poorer

"SO WHAT'S THE STORY ON THIS GUY?" MAXIMILIAN KUPPERMAN asked while peering over his glasses at his young assistant.

"Don't have too many details," said Jay. "Call came from Morris and Marks' office. According to their associate Arnold Kaplan, the guy is a potential bankruptcy client of the firm. Arnold said he advised the guy to talk to us first to see if we could help outside of court."

"Did he agree to do that?" Max asked. "And did Arnold point out to him we don't do this for free?"

Jay responded confidently. "Yes and yes. Howard Morris and his associates know as well as any law firm that you've got to get paid in this business. However, I believe Arnold told him he thought our policy was to spend as much time as we feel necessary, sometimes a lot of time, interviewing a potential client before requiring a retainer. I think he also said you were pretty selective about who you take on. As far as seeing us, I understand the guy seemed to jump at the chance to explore other options for getting out of whatever mess he is in without the stigma of a public bankruptcy filing, but . . ."

"But what?"

". . . but he wants us to meet him in his home. Wants as few people as possible knowing about his problem."

Heading out on their house call to meet the potential client, Jay drove and Max dozed.

Jay looked over from time to time at the old gentleman seated alongside him who was his mentor. Or, perhaps sometimes more like his tormentor. Except for the button down shirt, expensive tie, and suspenders he could pass for Moses or Abraham. Or, at times with the wire rimmed glasses and beard more like Father Christmas.

But Max was no jolly old simpleton. He always said, with only some exaggeration, that he had earned his gray hair the old-fashioned way, in the school of hard knocks. He also jokingly said that in order to be effective in crisis management work you had to be personally responsible for creating at least one major business crisis. One of his favorite preaching's was that you have to learn from adversity, that what separates the men from the boys was how well they applied take-away experiences to new challenges.

He enjoyed needling hotshot MBA's like Jay, whom he tended to dismiss as 'spreadsheet boys'. Although Max in fact had an excellent formal education, he liked to disarm others with the half-serious statement that he went to the *real* UCLA – not in Brentwood, but the University at the Corner of Lexington Avenue in New York City.

His point was, that often street smarts and real world experience counted for more than theoretical knowledge in the business arena. He would occasionally put down the pure academics by saying they had too much college and not enough high school.

He did concede that the ideal business toolkit was a combination of real experience in the trenches and theoretical training. He knew also that he was probably too old to acquire real proficiency in such arcane disciplines as quantitative analysis, predictive algorithms and behavioral heuristics. That's partly why he valued Jay so much, who not only could do spreadsheets backwards and forwards, but who had cutting edge formal training in the scientific side of business. So they made an effective team, Max's wide experience and judgment combined with the much younger man's energy, ambition and technical skills.

Leonard Babbitt lived not only on the good side of town, but on the Best Side of the Good Side. His house, like all the others in the neighborhood hid behind a wall and gated drive, reached only after being cleared through the entrance to the community by a security guard. After turning into Babbitt's driveway and buzzing the intercom, they pulled over to wait for the gate controller to operate.

"Notice anything unusual?" Max asked Jay.

"Just that all these monuments kinda look the same . . . they all scream money – what else?"

"They do scream money – but what kind of money?"

"OK, this sounds like one of your wisdom of the ages pronouncements coming . . . I'll bite. What kind?"

"Listen well wise guy, this is important. There are three kinds of money: old money, new money and temporary money. Old money is inherited, never earned. New money is earned or stolen. Temporary money is what you don't really own, just what you get the benefit of for a while – like the boyfriend of some CEO's ex-wife mooching off her property settlement until she kicks him out."

"I'll keep that in mind for when I become either a CEO or some rich gal's boyfriend. Now, what kind do we have around here?" asked Jay, genuinely interested in the answer.

"Maybe some temporary money, probably no old money. Sam Walton, or his heirs if they're smart, wouldn't be caught dead flaunting wealth like this. Besides the bad taste, it would make them a target for kidnapping, home invasions, and all the other you name it ugly stuff that we hear about nowadays.

"So that leaves earned or stolen," Max continued. "Oh, I should mention one other category. Won, as in winning the lottery or a poker tournament. But we can ignore those sources. Despite the media stories, real winners are so few and far between as to be almost non-existent."

He paused waiting for Jay to press the question.

"OK, let me guess, what we have here is a combination of earned and stolen."

"Right, but let's break it down a little more. Within the earned category we have money coming from the entertainment world, real operating businesses, and the professions. We can eliminate entertainment and sports personalities in this community – not a trendy enough area of Southern California. As far as professions, there could be a few high profile lawyers behind these walls, but no doctors. Even celebrity plastic surgeons don't earn enough to make a big splash around here. So, my young friend, I think what we are seeing is mostly the entrepreneurial ego drive of forty-something Captains of Industry manifested in ostentatious housing displays."

Jay was reminded once again of how much he admired the old man, how he always seemed to cut to the chase and make sense.

Max picked up with a final thought. "Of course, there is stolen money here too, or rather the proceeds from what are euphemistically called 'illicit activities'. Look at the black Cadillac Escalades and Lincoln Navigators tooling around, the drug lord vehicles of choice. Yep, for sure we have a few kingpins also living in this very upscale neighborhood."

Standing at the front door, Jay remembered he hadn't gotten an answer to what it was he was supposed to have noticed earlier. Max answered quickly.

"The ground cover needs weeding and trimming. No signs of a gardener working around here lately. There was a broken light on top of one of the gate columns. If the guy answers the door himself instead of the maid, we'll know."

"Know what?"

"He's in even bigger trouble financially than he told Morris and Marks."

"Good Morning. I'm Maximilian Kupperman and this is my

associate Jay Rosen."

"Hi, Lenny Babbitt, come in, come in. So you are the guys who are going to save my butt – right?" Babbitt said with immediate regret for his crudeness when he saw Max's weak smile.

"Let's get some information from you first, Mr. Babbitt."

"Sure, sure. By the way just call me Lenny. Are you Maximilian or just plain old Max?"

Jay smiled, knowing of Max's disdain for inappropriate familiarity.

"Actually I prefer Mr. Kupperman. But let's go with Max to save time. Why don't you begin by telling us what's going on – starting with your business activity."

"Yeah, uh, right. Where to begin? OK, I am in *Investment Banking*."

Jay jumped in. "Putting merger and acquisition deals together – an intermediary?"

Babbitt couldn't stop himself from making another clumsy attempt at humor. "No, let's say I *Make Investments and Bank the Obscene Profits*."

"Mr. Babbitt, uh, Leonard, we have limited time in which to conduct what we call a *Situation Analysis*. In a moment we will be discussing the fee we will be charging you if we get involved and, I assure you, at that point you will cut the comedy."

"Sorry, making light of things is my way of coping," said Babbitt contritely. "Here's the story."

Max listened and Jay took notes as Babbitt outlined what he did. He raised pools of money from private investors, which was then funneled into real estate loans secured by junior trust deeds, and business loans, secured by inventory and receivables, to borrowers with limited or zero creditworthiness. He also made equity investments in various ventures, usually ones with poor operating histories and risky profiles. As he explained it, high risk means high return and, over the years as the general partner in these deals he had personally done well, you might say very well.

Max's sideways glance at Jay conveyed it all – in this case it was sounding like Babbitt's *Investment Banking* was a code phrase for possible loan sharking, vulture funding, or similar activities all done out of a guy's office in his castle. Just like Gordon Gecko, but without the Wall Street overhead.

Babbitt went on to explain that one of his limited partnership funds had gotten embroiled in a big legal mess, resulting in new investor money drying up. So he was unable to make new deals. No new deals meant no income. No income meant – well, disaster. He was already facing big creditor pressure and having to use credit cards to cover his high living expenses.

Starting to perspire visibly, with both hands twitching nervously Babbitt blurted out, "I'll be honest with you guys. I have reviewed all of my alternatives and by far the most attractive is – *suicide!*"

Max paused, and deliberately, carefully, and even soothingly said, "Leonard, I've been in this business a long time. I've heard hundreds of stories and seen how almost every conceivable business problem can impact owners, managers, families, employees, suppliers, everybody. Trust me on this – no matter what kind of pressure you are under, unless you also have a terminal illness it should never warrant seriously *thinking* about the S word, much less actually pulling the trigger."

"You're not in my shoes," Babbitt protested.

"Right, I'm not. So put me in your shoes by detailing exactly what happened and where the real pressure is coming from."

So Babbitt began describing how, in his role as general partner, he had channeled one of his investment partnerships into a nursing home in Texas. After multiple and repeated violations, stemming largely from sloppy management, the institution was shut down by regulators. The fund went bust, with the limited partners losing their total investments.

"OK," said Max, "I understand. But limited partners know they can lose money, happens all the time. That's always clearly spelled out in the risk factors section of the original offering memorandum, sloppy management notwithstanding. Plus, as accredited investors they have to certify to being sophisticated enough to get it."

"True, all true. But . . . " Babbitt started to respond and paused. In his mind, Jay could hear the tape playing another of Max's truisms: *Whatever goes before the words but and except is a lie, and the real truth follows next.*

Babbitt went on. "I feel really stupid about this. As it turns out, we were kind of careless in putting the offering together. We talked to many more potential investors than the maximum number you are supposed to solicit, and most of the ones who put money in were just little people, not accredited."

"And now you are about to tell us this was not a registered offering and you are in trouble with both the SEC and state regulators?"

"Yeah, that's right. But it gets worse. The fact that we put these folks in an investment in another state makes it kind of like a kidnapper crossing state lines. I had to hire a securities defense lawyer to try to hold off the SEC, maybe negotiate a settlement. He tells me regardless of other outcomes, it's almost certain I'll be permanently barred from ever soliciting investor funds, even in limited private offerings done by the book."

"Alright, I see you are facing serious SEC issues but it sounds like the fines or penalties are yet to be imposed. So what immediate financial pressure led you to talk to a bankruptcy lawyer?"

"It's the Clark judgment," Babbitt almost whispered.

The details unfolded in messy progression. The Clarks were the sort of nice old couple featured in one of those AARP articles warning readers about *Losing Your Life Savings*. That was exactly what happened to them as limited partners in the nursing home failure. But the Clarks showed excellent judgment in their choice of attorney, who sued Babbitt and won.

"And who was representing you?" asked Max, already guessing the answer.

"Myron Glass, my wife's cousin. The same lawyer I used to put the original deal together. I've always used him."

Jay knew what Max was thinking: *Putz! You've already admitted your guy botched the partnership offering and exposed you to huge liability, and yet you use him to defend you in a lawsuit as important as this? How foolish.*

Controlling his rising irritation, Max simply asked, "you say there's a judgment. Judgment for what?"

"For fraud...and, uh...triple damages."

"What's the total?"

"Well, I, uh, can go get the exact amount from the file in my desk, but the Clarks' investment was $750,000. Times 3 is...what? Around $2.3 million. Oh, and they were also awarded attorneys' fees of $175,000." Yeah, thought Max and Jay simultaneously: *Sure, good lawyers are expensive – and there is a reason why. They win their cases.*

"So," continued Babbitt, "I guess the total including court costs is over $2.5 million."

Waiting for this to fully register with Max, Babbitt added, "so that's why I went to see Howard Morris – finally decided I have no choice but to file bankruptcy and get out from under."

Still restraining himself, Max asked slowly, "and what did Morris tell you?"

"I actually didn't talk much with him. He turned me right over to a young bankruptcy attorney in his office – Arnold, uh, Arnold Kaplan."

"And did Mr. Kaplan explain to you the applicability of seeking protection under the Federal Bankruptcy Code in your situation?"

"No, when I told him my situation was, uh pretty complicated with a lot of messy business and personal, uh ramifications, I guess is the word, he recommended I talk to you."

When Max drew up taller in his seat, Jay reflexively did the same and leaned forward to catch every word.

"Mr. Babbitt, fraud judgments, in common with fines and penalties for criminal acts, are not dischargeable in bankruptcy. When you are sued for fraud, a competent lawyer will always do four things. First, commence active discovery of the merits of the plaintiff's case. Second, realistically evaluate your defenses as the defendant, and the chances of the plaintiff prevailing. Third, open serious settlement negotiations if it looks as though you have real exposure."

"My God, you mean I can't - what was the fourth thing?"

"The fourth thing," continued Max in the professorial tone that Jay was so familiar with, "if settlement negotiations fail, is to immediately file a petition under Chapter 11 of the Bankruptcy Code."

"But you said bankruptcy wasn't an option for me!"

"It isn't now, but it was before. Please let me explain without interruption so we can move on."

Max continued and, in spite of the seriousness of the situation, somewhat enjoying delivering an almost detached discourse on a subject he knew very well.

He explained how, in spite of his broad powers, a Federal Bankruptcy Judge cannot set aside a fraud judgment rendered in state trial court. But if the case is still only pending in state court, a bankruptcy petition will stop it from proceeding, and require it to be litigated in Federal Bankruptcy Court.

"But why should that make any difference?" asked Babbitt.

"Because, the whole tenor of the Bankruptcy Court is the concept of a fresh start for the debtor. Plaintiffs don't always do as well arguing their cases in that venue. Even when they are nice people like the Clarks."

"So I'm really screwed." It was a statement, not a question.

"There is one other avenue to explore. From what you've told us, you probably have a malpractice case against your attorney, who apparently botched the private placement and blew the handling of the lawsuit. Depending on whether the statute of limitations has run, which in this state is one year from discovery, you might be able to sue him and hope the proceeds from his malpractice insurance are high enough to make the Clarks go away.

"But remember, you also have the other limited partners who lost big time to worry about – they are almost certain to pile on after the Clark judgment is recorded. I am actually surprised Clark's lawyer didn't try to get this certified as a class action. That's a lucky break for you."

Babbitt seemed to be more concerned about the idea of going after his own attorney. "You mean sue Myron Glass? Phyllis would never let me do that. He's family!"

"That's your call Leonard. It is not productive now to criticize your choice of legal representation or lecture you on the reason for the time-honored proscription against using family in these situations. I'm sure you realize all that now, after the fact. All Jay and I can do at this point is give our opinions and advice." Max started to get up and Jay knew the cue to put his yellow pad away and pick up his briefcase.

Babbitt remained seated at his desk, with eyes focused on another scene somewhere else, somewhere faraway.

"Please, gentlemen, sit down," he finally said earnestly. "I appreciate your efforts and respect your opinions, I really do. I would ask you to think about it, the whole mess, and get back to me with any other ideas. In the meantime there, uh is one more thing I have to get off my chest."

"And that is?"

"Phyllis, my wife."

Jay suppressed the possibly either provocative or comical image of Phyllis Babbitt, whom they had not met, on Babbitt's chest and glanced at Max, who ignored him and simply responded to Babbitt.

"What about your wife? Are there marital problems here as well?"

"No, no, not in that sense. But truthfully this is what really makes me think of suicide as the best way out."

Babbitt seemed now oddly at ease as he shared the story of his being married to Phyllis, wife number two, how she fit the image of what people call a Trophy Wife, how he had shielded her from details about his business activity, especially all the messy parts.

"You mean she knows nothing about the judgment, about the SEC problems? How can that be – her cousin was your attorney?"

"Myron knows I have desperately wanted to keep the lid on all this - plus he's embarrassed and really worried about his own skin, so he's had damn good reason to keep his mouth shut."

"Leonard, I have a long standing rule to not get involved in what transpires between a man and wife, if at all possible. But I also know from experience how closely intertwined business and domestic issues can be. And I can tell you the pressure that comes from hiding things like this from your loved ones can kill you, and I don't mean suicide, I mean ulcers, high blood pressure, nervous breakdown – you name it."

Babbitt now seemed closer himself to breaking down. "I don't think you could really understand, you probably have a wife you don't have to worry about impressing. You probably come from a totally different background."

"Leonard, let's get this out of the way. We are talking about you, not me. But if it's makes you more comfortable opening up, I will share some of my personal details.

"I was married for 43 years, my wife died not too long ago."

"God, I'm sorry, it's none of my . . ."

Max waved him off. "We had all the normal ups and downs. But I will tell you this, there was nothing *zilch* that she did not know about my professional activity or our financial condition. There is an overused term thrown around a lot these days, soul mate. I guess it means someone you can bare your soul to. And that is what Sarah and I had. She was proud of me sure, but the bottom line was she loved me for myself, in spite of what I had or had not accomplished. And that is what makes it possible to get through whatever life throws in your face."

"Max, uh," Babbitt stammered, "I don't know what to . . ."

"Let me wrap this up. As to my background, both sets of my grandparents were born in a small village in eastern Europe. You've seen one just like it in *Fiddler on the Roof*. Like thousands of other immigrant Jews they settled in Brooklyn. No money, but they possessed the same traits as nearly all the millions of immigrants who came through Ellis Island in those days – dreams of a better life, work ethic, concern for family, passion for education, and frugality. My grandfather and my father both preached: *Watch the pennies and the dollars will take care of themselves.* I have to say around this neighborhood it looks more like the mantra is: *Spend the dollars and who cares if we wind up with pennies*. One more thing. Dad always stressed the importance of keeping *both* business *and* personal overhead low. He knew instinctively that when your nut is small, all your options remain open. And when it's high, you put yourself in a real tight corner with few or no alternatives."

Max was moving quickly now, wanting to conclude his narrative. Jay was listening as intently as Babbitt, even though he had heard most of the story before.

"My father had a food business that eventually expanded throughout New York City. But in spite of his financial success, he and my mother remained living in the same somewhat dilapidated brownstone in the same lower middle class area of Brooklyn for the rest of their lives. Drove the same used Buick for at least 15 years. I grew up there, went to PS 104 in the same neighborhood, high school at Brooklyn Tech; then Brooklyn College, NYU for a master's in Corporate Finance, and finally Columbia Law. I had my own costly foray in the world of private enterprise, initially as an outside investor, then part owner in a startup venture that failed. Took me only six weeks to get in but two years to get out. Lost some serious money, but learned some very valuable real world lessons that have served me well working with clients over the years. Joined a big New York law firm, became a partner and did a lot of general corporate work, then insolvency legal work, a lot of it very complicated and challenging. Eventually moved to California and started this specialized consulting practice.

"NOW LEONARD – why haven't you told your wife the truth?"

Caught off guard by Max's abrupt return to the problem at hand, Babbitt began stammering again. "Well, Phyllis, she uh, please, can I first share some things about how we live around here?"

It was like listening to a documentary program on National Public Radio as Babbitt chronicled what life was like in his world from his perspective. The chronic conspicuous consumption, the desperate social climbing and one-upmanship, the spoiled rotten kids with their own personal trainers and private soccer coaches.

"Here's a true story, Max - I have a friend at the country club who is an investment banker – a REAL Investment Banker, not a phony like me." Babbitt smiled as his own dig at himself produced the same reaction in his two listeners.

"Anyway, David comes from a pretty modest background, worked hard to get to where he is at his firm. He's been worried for some time about his 10 year old son being way too materialistic and kind of growing away from him. So he decided it was time for a father-son bonding experience, doing some physical labor together, a lesson in real values." He paused to make sure he got David's story exactly right.

"They went to the little boutique nursery here in the village, bought a tree for probably three times what Home Depot would charge, shovels and fertilizer, and went home to start digging a hole to plant the thing. As David tells it, his son makes a couple of feeble attempts to uncover some soil and then stops after only a minute or so.

"Hey Dad," says the boy, "this is WAY too hard. Let's hire some wetback to do it and I'll pay for it."

As Babbitt recalled it, his friend didn't know whether to laugh or cry at first, and was very angry when he found out how much 'walking around money' the kid's mother had been funneling to the boy. Of course, her defense was the old 'every other family does the same thing' – you wouldn't want Ritchie to not have what the other kids do, would you?'

Babbitt followed with other anecdotes, piling up evidence that proved to him he was trapped in a pretty sick society.

"But I'm as bad as everyone else. For a long time we have been in over our heads and I haven't had the guts to admit it – not to my golfing buddies, not to my business contacts – and especially not to Phyllis. I have made a lot of money over the years but our expenses have always seemed to rise at a faster rate. I feel like the hamster running in the wheel. But the wheel just stopped, we're broke and I AM ASHAMED!"

Jay settled as deep as possible in the chair, his trademark flippancy evaporated. He was party to the worst scene a chronic wisecracker could face – real heart-wrenching emotion. He was about to see a man cry. He hoped Max would jump in quickly – after all the old man was the world champion moralizer, equal to any situation like this.

Head in his hands, Babbitt gushed, "but I'm not just broke, I'm broke with dishonor. I am now a pariah. I've let everyone down, especially Phyllis. Her Lexus is going to be repossessed any day now. Next time she tries using her credit card on Rodeo Drive or at the spa it will probably be rejected. Myron warned me what to expect. As soon as the Clark judgment is recorded, and the SEC findings hit the financial press, my credit score goes sub-zero. On top of everything else, the IRS and maybe the FBI could then be knocking at the door."

Sounds of a car in the driveway announced the arrival of Phyllis, home from her morning tennis match. Jay saw the Lexus outside and, reverting to sarcastic form thought to himself: *Well, at least Mr. Repo man didn't get the hook on it yet.*

"What's going on Len – who are these gentlemen?" asked Phyllis, trying to be civil but annoyed at finding strangers in her home.

Babbitt made the introductions and simply said, "honey, I have an awful lot to tell you. I'm hoping Mr. Kupperman and Mr. Rosen will stand by to help me get through what I have to say."

After Babbitt had struggled through his true confession, Phyllis said slowly, with emphasis, "Len, I am mad at you. Not for what has happened, but for leaving me out of it. Believe it or not, I care deeply for you and I am your life partner. Partners are supposed to share everything.

"And how stupid do you think I am? Do you put me in the same category as the air-headed bimbos married to some of your friends? When the process server shows up at the house with papers and you dismiss it as 'just some business documents,' I'm supposed to buy that? When Myron avoids talking to me when I visit Aunt Sheila, when you tell me the two of you keep having to attend a series of meetings in Century City to 'wrap up a new deal,' you think I don't know it's got to be more than that?"

Finally she reached her conclusion. "Here's the crazy part Len, you think I enjoy this lifestyle, the club, the cars, the socializing, the trips to Vail and Palm Beach, the jewelry, the toys? It's all BS. My so-called girlfriends are almost all bitchy, neurotic backstabbers. Like your fair-weather buddies, they will have nothing to do with me or you when the news breaks. But you know what honey? That's fine with me. I could live under a bridge if . . . " Phyllis paused, " . . . if only if we were living under there together."

They all talked for a while about action steps. There was no question the house would go on the market immediately. Leonard and Phyllis still had maybe low to medium seven figure equity in their home, even in a down real estate market, and Max thought there might be a good chance of settling with the Clarks and avoiding judgment debtor examinations and writs of attachment. There could be enough in the pot to spread around the other investors and keep them from suing. Max also thought that Babbitt's SEC lawyer could probably get the penalties for securities violations mitigated by demonstrating good faith efforts to make restitution. Max threw Babbitt another life line by telling him he would research some contacts around the country that might help him make a fresh start. Through all of this, Phyllis was energized and upbeat. It was contagious, and when she said, "well, I am going upstairs now to see what jewelry I can pawn and start packing," even Babbitt laughed.

Standing at the front door Babbitt said to Max, "I remember Arnold Kaplan telling me you guys are the best and don't work for nothing. If you let me know what I owe you, I can put it on my American Express Card while I'm still able."

"Forget it, Len, right now seeing you and Phyllis working together is our reward. We'll stay in touch."

"Max…thank you, thank you," Babbitt said, now really teary eyed as they embraced. "You know what you have done? You - *you have saved my life.*"

They drove quietly back downtown, both absorbed in thought.

"So Boss, did you check out Mrs. B. in her tennis outfit?"

"Christ, Jay. That's all we need – you lusting after a potential client's wife," Max muttered. "Leave it to you to taint being witness to a true epiphany - a ruined man redeeming himself by admitting his failure and weakness, and facing the music. I guess it's fortunate we won't be taking on a formal assignment – I won't have to worry about you complicating things. Maybe one of these days you'll get a steady girlfriend and have an outlet for your overactive libido. And maybe one of these days I'll stop letting you drag me down to your level with conversation like this."

"Sorry Boss, you're right about the important truths we have seen affirmed today. It reminds me of the Alcoholic Anonymous 12 step program. You know - first stand up and admit to the world that you have a big problem."

"Exactly," confirmed Max.

"But I can't stop thinking about the AA 13 step program."

"Haven't heard of that – what is it?"

"That's when you start sleeping with someone you met during the 12 steps."

"Always the wise guy." Max said with a weak smile.

2

A Nice Friendly Banker

ROBERT, I'D LIKE YOU TO MEET PAUL ARROWSMITH, THAT IS, Dr. Arrowsmith. Paul, this is Robert Patterson," said Max warmly.

"Nice to meet you Doctor – are you a physician?" asked Robert.

"Gosh, no, just an egghead scientist," Paul said somewhat sheepishly. "And please, it's Paul."

Max smiled and said, "nobody with a Ph.D. in Molecular Biology out of MIT can ever be described as *just* an anything," then added, "I was introduced to Paul by Gordon Jacobson. You know Gordon, Robert?"

"The Silicon Valley guru? Just by reputation – we've never actually met," said Robert.

"Anyway Robert, Paul has an interesting situation he is looking at and could really use a veteran banker's input."

Robert laughed. "Veteran as in an old war horse about to be

put out to pasture."

"Don't let him kid you, Paul. This guy still throws an awful lot of weight around in the financial world. Why don't you bring him up to speed?"

"Sure. And let me just say, Robert, how much I appreciate your taking the time to visit. And, of course thanks to Max for setting this lunch up," he paused, then continued. "For about the last five years I have been chief scientist for an area biotech firm. In the last year or so I've been concerned that my efforts aren't going to pay off for me financially – my stock options are underwater. We have pretty solid IP but ownership has made some disastrous business decisions and it is looking as though any successful merger or IPO is probably way down the road.

"Anyway, I am bound by the usual contract that assigns ownership of any new patents I develop to the company. I feel at this point in my life I need to be the one to get royalties from whatever I invent. So I'm thinking about getting involved in a new business."

Robert commented, "before hearing more, let me just offer the caution that the commercialization of new ideas is almost always long, difficult and expensive. Typically, successfully bringing a new product to market costs ten times what it did to do the R&D leading up to the proof of concept. And of course, without proof of concept you have nothing."

Paul responded, "yes, I guess I kind of knew that, even though the economics of business in general are sure not my area of expertise."

Max jumped in. "You don't have to *know* the answers, you have to know where to *get* the answers."

Paul smiled. "Right, that's what my friend Gordon said, and that's why he got me together with Max."

He went on. "Well, I know this guy who owns a boutique medical devices development company who wants me to hook up with him. He says I'll manage the research and development and together we'll do the marketing or licensing of the products."

"What is the proposed relationship?" asked Robert.

"Well, besides doing the R&D I'm supposed to kick in cash for working capital and he is contributing the existing business. We will own the new entity fifty-fifty. So what I need from you Robert, is some guidance on how to finance this thing."

"Paul, besides the obvious issue of putting a realistic value on the business and what the respective contributions of the partners would be, I strongly advise you to get professional advice on the structure, the business plan, and the many issues that need to be addressed on the front end to avoid problems on the back end – all areas that Kupperman & Company is certainly expert in. Max here is also the one to help you with the fundamental, critical question of debt versus equity. As far as the mechanics of bank borrowing to finance a business, I can give you a short course," said Robert.

"But first let me mention what I *won't* be covering, and that is SBA loans. As you may know, these are loans that are 90% guaranteed by the government through the Small Business Administration. A lot of the smaller banks will steer you in that direction because, although they fund the loan, they only have 10% at risk - the SBA guarantees 90%. Is there a place for them? Sure, but the paperwork can be daunting, and the limitations, restrictions and covenants hard to live with. It would definitely be an avenue for you to consider if you were buying a convenience store or auto repair business, particularly if there was real estate involved, but not as a way to finance what I call a 'real business'. OK?"

Paul nodded yes and Robert continued. "But first I would like to briefly discuss the latest finance craze - *Crowdfunding* . . . have you heard about that?"

Paul had a blank stare. "Gosh no - what the heck is that?"

Chuckling, Robert briefly described the 2012 JOBS Act that allows small businesses to raise capital through online websites. "This has become the hot new thing in grass roots business finance. People are raising money on the internet for some really off the wall projects. You are bound to hear more and more about this approach as it gains traction. In fact, by the time we finish lunch there will probably be a bunch of new websites open that do this."

Intrigued, both Paul and Max looked at Robert who continued. "Here's an example of how it works. Let's say you are a couple in a college town who have an idea for a health food store. You figure you need about $25K to open up. One of these web-based outfits will publicize your plan and collect "donations" from the public in "units" as little as 25 bucks each. When the "investors" make their payment to the intermediary online, they also acknowledge on the website that they understand the return of their money is contingent on the venture being successful, and that they might never get a dime back."

"Wow, this is new stuff for me too - is this really legal Robert?" asked Max.

"Right now, yes. But there are many legitimate questions and concerns about the whole concept, not the least of which is the usual absence of detailed financial statements, and no operating history in most cases. So it is really impossible to evaluate risk.

And without knowing risk, you can't determine pricing. The SEC is yet to issue its final guidelines and regulations about what's legal and what's not. When it does, there will be a big shakeout and a lot of money changing hands with, of course, the litigation that always follows. I'd suggest Paul, that for now you forget you've ever heard of *Crowdfunding*."

"No worries there - I'm too conservative by nature to be on the cutting edge. Except of course when it comes to scientific research."

They all smiled, and Robert then went on by recounting his career in commercial banking, which had culminated in his becoming Regional Vice President for one of the big banks, in one of the country's largest banking regions, with overall responsibility for almost 160 branches, or banking centers as they were now known.

"Let me tell you how banking has changed," he was warming up to a discussion about something he knew well and enjoyed talking about. "In the old days, before the S&L crisis and scandals over deals made by good old boys in Georgia, Texas and Arkansas, we used to make character loans. For many years I had a personal lending limit of one million dollars without having to go to the loan committee. That meant I could loan you seven-figures on my sole authority with just your signature IF I had a good feeling about you. And my sixth sense about that was very rarely off target. In other words, besides the normal collateralized business lines of credit, I made unsecured character loans, lots of them."

"Then what happened?" asked Paul.

"They hauled off all the characters making character loans," answered Robert, and the three laughed.

He went on. "Seriously, today virtually all loans are now made using scoring done remotely by someone who doesn't know you. If you don't fit in the right box in the matrix you are out of luck. Sure, a local loan officer still . . . uh . . . question Paul?"

"Yeah, sorry Robert - what exactly do you mean by scoring and matrix?"

"My apologies for throwing some of these industry terms around without explanation," answered Robert. "It is pretty simple actually. Imagine a worksheet with columns and rows that have labels for criteria that are important to making a decision about creditworthiness. Think about when you filled out an application for a car loan, credit card or home mortgage. For a business loan the information you provide is entered in the appropriate box on the scoring matrix. Each of the criteria has a point value and is weighted by its relative importance in evaluating credit. For example, a FICO score over 800 and long length of time on the job might each warrant matrix scores of 9 on a scale of 1 to 10. Being just out of school and renting instead of owning your own home might only get you one or two points.

"The bank will total up your score on the matrix and compare it to what it knows about the likelihood of you performing as agreed, based on its experience with thousands, or even millions of similar loans. Does that help Paul?"

"Absolutely, thanks Robert."

"Good. As I was saying, a local loan officer still does the write-up, assembles all the supporting material and sends it to committee, but the process is now essentially impersonal. And that is probably a good thing."

Paul, listening intently, then asked, "so what does one need to borrow money for a business nowadays?"

"Let me answer by first pointing out the change in requirements mandated by government regulators, which is actually another good thing. Essentially all business lines of credit now have to be supported by a write-up that analyzes the three principal sources of repayment – *primary*, *secondary* and *tertiary*. *Primary* is cash flow from the business itself. *Secondary* is what would be available if business assets were liquidated. *Tertiary* is what the bank would get at the end of the day by seizing and liquidating personal assets of individuals who have signed personal guarantees."

"What exactly is a personal guarantee?" Paul asked innocently, as Max thought to himself: *Oh boy, this poor guy really is out of his element, a typical academic babe in the business woods.*

Robert responded patiently. "When you sit down later with Max, I'm certain he will go over the possible forms of business structure and confirm this cardinal rule – *never do business as an individual*. This is especially important if your products or services involve third parties who could have claims against you. Your only practical choice is to set up either a regular corporation or a LLC, a Limited Liability Company, both of which provide a shield between business liability claims and your personal assets. Then the only thing you can lose is your actual investment in the business, not your house."

"That makes sense – but what is this guarantee business?" Paul persisted.

"I'm coming to that. The bank is smart, so the only way you are going to get a loan is to sign a personal guarantee, in effect waiving your protection under the corporate shield, putting all your personal assets at risk and giving the bank a right to sell your home if the business goes bust."

"Jeez, that's bad," Paul said, now sounding depressed.

"It is what it is, my friend. And that's why ninety-plus percent of folks would rather work for a paycheck that they receive from somebody else, than stay awake worrying about their exposure on a business loan. But, hey, it is the old story, life itself is fraught with risk – we accept it, we manage it, and we strive to achieve commensurate rewards. That's the essence of entrepreneurship."

"Yes, I see that. But could you back up and tell me more about the other sources of loan repayment – what were they...uh, primary and...secondary?"

"Correct, and of the two the primary is by far the most important, since it is what results from the business being successful. Remember the bank doesn't want to take over the business assets and they don't want to have to move against your or a relative's personal assets under the guarantee. They want you to make it. Now we get to the key point – you are not going to get the loan unless the bank is satisfied that the business is going to produce sufficient cash to meet all its business needs AND pay the loan back," said Robert with emphasis.

"So what is going to satisfy the bank on that score?" Paul asked.

"Think about it," answered Robert, "the best predictor of future success is always past success. Like with the human animal, where the best predictor of future behavior is always past behavior. Just as the case with every woman who marries a bum thinking he would change, and then discovers to her dismay that he is still a drunk, cheat or abuser. Can people ever change? Sure, it *can* happen but it is statistically far safer to bet it won't. Max, I know you would agree with this, right?"

"Absolutely, and I would like to share a little true story on this issue of change if I may, because it is such an important point," Max said earnestly, and then went on.

"Many years ago I became friends with a brilliant young physician I will refer to as Doc. He was first in his class at Johns Hopkins, triple board certified in internal medicine, neurology and psychiatry.

"As is common with a lot of smart dedicated scientists, Doc started out wanting to change the world, make it better, serve humanity. He and his wife Janet were both interested in working with what is called the underclass, especially minorities. Doc later became focused on the challenges involved in rehabilitating criminals, so he went on and got a lot of specialty training in understanding the criminal mind and sociopathic behavior.

"He received an assignment as the resident psychiatrist at one of the California medium security prisons, got to work with a lot of the inmates, and then started concentrating on a handful that seemed to have the most potential to rejoin society.

"From the start one of his biggest challenges was dealing with the skepticism of the prison guards and staff. One day he asked the warden for permission to have social contact with a couple of the inmates, in a family setting, feeling that even limited exposure to the way 'normal,' responsible folks live would help even the hard cases along the rehabilitation path.

"The warden thought he was naive, but went along with the scheme after insuring that adequate security was in place. So then one evening, Janet and Doc played host to two relatively clean-cut convicts at dinner in their home. You know what happened?" Max asked his friends.

"My God, don't tell me they were murdered and the cons escaped!" exclaimed Paul, as both he and Robert braced themselves for the reply.

"No, nothing that dramatic," answered Max, "but in the long run, in a way, almost worse." He went on to relate that after the convicts and guards left their home to return to the prison facilities that evening, Janet discovered that some of her best silverware pieces were missing, amazingly swiped right under their noses.

"Janet protested to Doc that she could hardly believe it – the young inmates had seemed so polite, so grateful to have a chance to get out in another world for a pleasant evening. From that moment on, Doc realized that the first syllable in the noun convict is very apt: *con* – that's what they do, that's all most of them will ever do. Developed to an extreme, they could become a Ted Bundy, the con artist and charmer *par excellence*, the ultimate sociopath. For Doc the evening was an epiphany, a revelation that started him down a new path.

"Doc went on to become a giant in the field of researching the criminal mind and behavior. He didn't have much interest in solving crimes, which always fascinates the general public, but rather in exploring the causes. He well knew the scientific dictum that says *find the cause and you have found the solution*. He was widely published, in demand at conferences, and enjoyed broad international peer respect. Except in one area."

"What was that?" asked Robert.

"His unwavering belief in the sociological theories x and y, which go to the heart of the 'change is possible' idea."

"What are theories x and y?" asked Paul.

"Briefly, that there are good guys and there are bad guys in society. The good guys by and large stay good their whole lives, and the bad guys create continual problems for themselves and everybody else as long as they live. It is the same belief that the police and most other law enforcement professionals adopt sooner or later."

"Actually sounds pretty reasonable to me," Robert commented. "Who would have a lot a trouble with the idea?"

"First, most mental health practitioners. If changing human behavior isn't easy or even possible, a lot of analysts are out of a job. Second, all the self help gurus who pack in the folks at seminars, sell their books and CDs, then pack the same folks back in at another seminar when they fall back to their old ways. Finally, the average person, who wants to believe there is always hope, regardless of the evidence staring them in the face. For them the notion is too fatalistic, smacks too much of genetic pre-determination, which doesn't go down very well in the Western world."

"What happened to Doc, what's he doing now?" Robert asked.

"He became a consultant to Interpol, the FBI and a couple of the big city police departments. As far as his ideas on the prison population, he caught a lot of flak by maintaining that society would be better off abandoning rehabilitation efforts and diverting the resources to helping the best and brightest of the underclass to get in, and stay in, the theory x group, the good guy herd. He was passionate about the value of higher education and always cited the tragic statistic that there are more black men in prison than in colleges and universities in the U.S. He always remained skeptical however, about the importance of nurture in the Nature vs. Nurture controversy, feeling that in the end, like breeding race horses, genetics always wins out. A few years back he came out with his definitive final answer to the 'is real change possible?' question," said Max, slowly, with effect.

"And the answer is?" asked Paul expectantly.

"Doc would say that there are three ways that real change in human behavior is possible. The first is a lifetime of psychotherapy – not a month or a year, but every week for the rest of one's life. The second is a true religious conversion – not falling for a TV evangelist, but actually moving to a monastery on a mountain top in Tibet and spending the rest of your life in contemplation with your fellow monks. But he would say the third way is the only one that is guaranteed to succeed . . . "

"What's the third?" Robert and Paul asked almost simultaneously.

"*A frontal lobotomy.*"

There was a long pause as the narrative sunk in. Finally Robert offered, "Max, all I can say is, that is an amazing story about a remarkable man. Not sure I would agree entirely with his thesis, but I would love to meet him. How do you know so much about him?"

"Janet is my sister. Doc was my brother-in-law. He died some years back, way too young. Thanks for letting me make that detour guys – it's a subject that I have been pretty wrapped up in for a long time. Now it's time for Robert to get us back on track."

After taking a break for fresh air on the patio outside, the three men sat back down and Robert picked up where he had left off.

"If you are an established business, your track record over time is easy to prove up. If you have a history of growing top line revenue and strong bottom line earnings, and your industry position is favorable, you are about to join that exclusive club whose members are known as *Prime Credit Risks*."

"But," Paul asked, "what if you are a start-up without a history, or have a weak track record?"

"I'd like to hold off addressing that for a moment," answered Robert, "but first I have just mentioned the 'C' word – Credit, and I'd like to get more into that. Have you ever heard the phrase *The Three C's of Credit?*"

"No - I don't think I have . . . "

Robert went on, "I want to elaborate a bit here because it is another example of how lending and, I suppose, society in general has changed. The Three C's are *Character, Capacity,* and *Collateral.* Let's take *Character* first. It is the moral element. It is pride, it is integrity. It is being true to your word, it is honoring your commitments no matter what."

"I understand," said Paul. "Like what you said earlier about when you made character loans to people you knew you could trust. But that sounds like a subjective determination – how can you quantify something like that?"

"To limit the discussion to lending criteria, and leave the big 'meaning of life' question to wise old philosophers like my good friend here," answered Robert with a generous nod to Max, "the answer is simple – what your credit report says about you. The way you have handled your financial obligations in the past is the number one measure of Character for credit purposes."

Trying to anticipate where Robert was heading Paul asked,

"well I would imagine that is the most important of the criteria, because it goes to the moral issue, right?"

"Excellent observation, Paul – and in days gone by you would have been correct. But this is my point about how things have changed. Now it is all about *Capacity* – your ability to pay the money back. In other words, it doesn't matter so much what your intentions are if you don't have the proverbial pot to piss in. Look at the FICO score components – you know about FICO scores, right?"

Paul nodded yes.

"Well," Robert went on, "the geniuses who developed these scoring algorithms determined that if what you owe is a high percentage of your available credit, that really should count heavily against you in assessing credit risk. In other words, you could have made every payment on time over many years, but if you are currently up against your limit on credit card use, you will find your FICO score tanking. The actual way they compute your score these days is that the amount of your debt combined with the *type* of the debt accounts for the biggest chunk of your score. Just like cholesterol, there is good debt and bad debt, and bad debt is unsecured credit card use. Again, these guys are smart – they know no matter how badly you might want to pay, without disposable income and access to liquid resources you are probably using credit cards to survive and in danger of default. And, if you carefully peruse your credit file you will notice it contains principally data relating to payment history and debt as reported by lenders – there is nothing about your assets. That's because the lenders actually don't care what your stated assets are. It's a classic *a priori* situation – requiring no further investigation or proof, because they figure if you really possessed good tangible assets, you wouldn't be borrowing money at a 24% APR."

Paul, looking almost annoyed said, "boy, I guess it is true what I have always heard – the only way you can get a loan is if you can prove you don't need the money."

Robert smiled. "To a large extent that is true. But to defend the geniuses I just referred to in a somewhat disparaging tone, credit scoring is a real breakthrough because it moves decision making from subjective to objective and quantifies risk. Anytime you can make a decision based on mathematical probability you are better off. I think it was Damon Runyon who said *'the race isn't always won by the swift and the sure – but that's the way you want to bet'*. If the bank finds out you just lost your job, it knows the odds of you defaulting on your obligations just went up, regardless of what a sterling fellow you have always been. Again – and I can't stress this enough – it is *capabilities, not intentions* that matter most in the end. That doesn't count just in lending, it's a principle understood by savvy governments and military leaders down through the ages. What won World War II for the allies was the tremendous industrial *capacity* of America. But to get back to banking, it helps to keep in mind the competing forces in play in the lending business. Banks have assets, in the form of their own capital and funds from depositors. Those assets have to be put to work, have to earn a return. The trick is to balance risk against reward. If you want to get that loan on reasonable terms you must convince the bank that you are a reasonable risk. I'll talk about ways to do that in a moment, but first let's have some more coffee and then I'd like to go over the third criteria, *Collateral*."

As the coffee cups were being filled Max thought how fortunate he was to know men like Robert – smart, experienced and genuinely willing to share. He looked over at Paul and had the impression of a scientist assimilating the results of an important discovery, which was in fact exactly the case.

"Any questions at this point, Paul?"

"Uh, I'm still digesting all this, Robert, thanks. I'm sure I'll have some when you're finished."

"OK, let's try to wrap this up," said Robert. "From the lender's perspective, the key question in looking at collateral is the extent to which it's *fungible*. By fungible in this context we mean how readily we can dispose of the collateral; how quickly and at what price we can unload the assets backing up the loan. A car loan is the best example I can give – if you default, the lender can move quickly to yank that car right out from under your nose and dispose of it readily, with minimum expense. In contrast, if the collateral consists of specialized equipment, obsolete inventory, or questionable receivables it's a whole different situation, and the bank knows it might only get pennies on the dollar. If you are the borrower in that case, you better be prepared to have your personal assets attached under the guarantee we discussed earlier. Still with me Paul?"

Paul smiled weakly. "Yeah, but I do have kind of a queasy feeling in my stomach about all of this right about now."

Robert laughed. "You sound like a condemned prisoner. It doesn't need to be all doom and gloom. Let's finish with how to get that loan."

He continued, "but one more thing for you to know about is the role of the regulators. Remember the bank has its own underwriting criteria that it uses to make the loan in the first place. But its loan portfolio is subject to examination by both state and federal examiners who can force the bank to classify a loan as marginal or worse, a bad risk, non-performing. When that happens the bank may have to write-off the loan and charge it against its bad debt reserves. That's bad for the bank, bad for the borrower, and potentially bad for the entire banking system, if the problems are widespread. By the way, here's a tip – *always stay close to the loan officer at the bank who did the initial write up and oversees your loan*. And never lie, try to hide bad news, or dodge phone calls. That loan officer has a vested interest in making sure that your loan isn't classified or written off, because if it is, that's potentially a black mark against him or her. While a loan is still performing the officer has something to say about what happens. But when it is classified as non-performing, the loan usually goes to the folks at 'special assets'. That's the department in the bank that is concerned about only one thing, recovering as much as possible from liquidating business assets and what they can squeeze from guarantors. As the owner, you are out of business at that point and better be talking to Kupperman & Company about ways to salvage enough to start a new life."

"I think we've given Paul enough of a reality check at this point – and probably scared him to boot," Max said smiling. "Now let's tell him what he needs to know to improve his chances of getting that loan and avoid the problem issues."

"Thanks, Max," said Robert, then continuing, "it all comes down to a credible plan – the *primary* source of repayment I mentioned earlier, cash flow from the business itself. I remember in the early days of my career I would ask a small businessman sitting across from me 'so how much money do you need?'. And he would answer 'as much as I can get'. That was typical. And it wasn't meant as just a flippant answer, it was an indication of a dangerous level of ignorance about his own business."

Robert went on. "It's *your* job as the business owner or senior executive to know what your working capital needs are. So we are back to how critical the financial plan is. It is a fact that most business failures are due to lack of planning, not lack of money. And we are not talking about a marketing plan, though that is certainly important. We are talking about a *detailed cash flow forecast.*"

"By cash flow you mean profits?" asked Paul.

"No, no . . . NO," answered Robert emphatically. "You can success yourself right out of business by generating lots of sales, and ignoring the need for cash to support increased receivables, inventory and so forth. Remember *growing sales and paper profits do not automatically translate into cash in the bank.*"

"Uh, I guess this is a stupid question - but how do you determine cash flow?" asked Paul, sounding somewhat embarrassed by his need to keep asking for basic answers.

"That's not that difficult," answered Robert. "Your business accounting software will be able to generate cash flow reports, but they will generally be based on *historic* data. What we are talking about is a credible forecast of *future* results, and that is best laid out using a separate spreadsheet program."

"Boy, I don't think I have the skills to be able to do that myself," said Paul.

"Right, but a capable controller or accounting manager should, and there are consultants out there who can help. But I should warn you about consultants," Robert paused, smiling at Max, "a lot of time the label 'consultant' is a code word for *unemployed, waiting for a real job*. Also, it is a lot easier to find a consultant in areas like marketing, human resources, website design and so forth, than one who really knows managerial accounting, finance, and forecasting. Would you agree Max?"

"Right on Robert," Max answered with a grin. "Find me a real job and I'll give up this consulting stuff."

They all smiled as Robert said, "no you won't, because then I would no longer have somebody to help turnaround the bank's worst problem loans."

Robert looked around to see if there was a write-on wipe-off board on the wall of the lounge at the country club where they were having lunch. Seeing there wasn't, he took a legal pad out of his briefcase and asked Paul to sit close to him.

"I want to sketch out for you the format of the kind of forecast I like to see," he said.

He marked out the months of the year across the top of the page, and wrote a series of labels down the left side.

"You see how this works," he said to Paul, "the top row is net income by month. This data actually feeds in from a detailed income and expense schedule that would be another part of the spreadsheet. But for now I want to concentrate on the cash flow."

He went on to explain how the 'paper income' had to be adjusted to account for actual monies collected from customers, the timing of payments to suppliers, and the outgoes for salaries and other operating expenses. Then he talked about adding back non-cash expenses like depreciation.

"I'm confused," said Paul. "Why would depreciation not be an expense? Or maybe I don't know what depreciation is . . ."

Answering as simply as he could, Robert gave the example of the business having to invest in lab equipment or production machinery, and then being able to 'write off' a portion of the original cost each year of the expected life of the asset.

"The amount that is written off each year is a non-cash expense because we already used cash when we bought it in the first place, but the accounting rules say we can't deduct the whole investment cost at once. So even though it is an expense for financial statement purposes, for cash flow purposes, a part of it is added back to income in the current accounting period. But if we buy new equipment in that period, that then is a *new* cash requirement that *reduces* our cash flow. But this is what I want to really leave you with. You see here that the report has a beginning bank balance and an ending bank balance after making all of these adjustments to our paper profits each month. If the ending balance is negative – an overdraft – it has to be made up somehow. And the somehow is either new money from shareholders or, preferably a working capital line of credit from a lender that can be drawn down on to cover the shortfall and paid back when there is a surplus. Over the course of the year this kind of format will show the maximum line of credit needed by the business and exactly when it can be repaid.

"That's why we bankers love it – it answers the question 'how much do you need' in a logical, quantified way and tells those of us on the other side of the desk that you as the owner know the financial side of your business and how to keep score."

Robert stood and said, "time to get back to that desk now. Best of luck in your all your endeavors, Paul. Let me know how things work out and if I can help in any way."

Paul shook his hand and almost stammered, "I can't thank both of you enough, Robert and I, uh . . . "

"It was my pleasure, Paul. Oh by the way," he added, "if my bank ever loans you money I am going to have to charge you a higher interest rate than usual."

"Why is that?" asked Paul.

"Because now you know all an old banker's secrets."

3

What A Great Place To Work

"WOULD YOU GENTLEMEN LIKE TO HEAR ABOUT OUR SELECTION of gourmet coffee?" inquired the attractive, immaculately groomed young lady with perfect teeth. "We are quite proud of what we have available in our lounge – better than Starbucks."

"Thanks, but I'm fine with ordinary brewed or even instant, answered Max, "how about you Jay?"

"Same here," said Max's associate as the two men began scanning the waiting room.

"Mr. Krantz will be with you shortly," said Miss Perfect Teeth as she placed the two cups and saucers on the inlaid coffee table and then left.

"Bone china, Jay. Usually we would be served ordinary mugs or even Styrofoam cups."

"Right, Boss, and you will be proud of me for noticing the original art on the walls and works of sculpture on the corner tables. You know what that tells me?"

Max paused in his reply as a man and woman wearing building services uniforms entered the lobby, carrying various maintenance items. One started dusting and spraying each individual leaf on the potted plants, while the other vacuumed the inside walls of what was at least a thousand gallon salt water fish tank taking up one entire wall of the lobby.

After the plant and fish tank couple moved down the hall to service the individual executive offices, Max asked Jay, "ok, what does it tell you?"

"That management has money to burn, is really image conscious. By the way, since we drove here separately and couldn't talk in the car, I'm not exactly sure what our mission is here at CCI."

"I'll get to that in a moment Jay, but when you dig into the history of Computer Concepts Inc., you'll see that they used to be located in Corona, in Riverside County, where the cement plants and low overhead industrial and distribution operations are. And you were spot on in your observation. We are now sitting in a plush office in Newport Beach, the highest of the high rent districts, while downstairs the most expensive labor in Southern California is assembling and shipping product. *Why*?"

"Uh. . .Jerry Krantz likes to surf? Wants to be close to good seafood restaurants? Or maybe they lost their lease on the Corona facility - I don't know. What do you think?" asked Jay.

"I think there is NO good business reason for them moving here. The products are sold in stores like Staples and Office Depot, distribution channels that don't care where the headquarters and manufacturing is located. They still do assembly here in the US instead of sourcing from Asia. It is way too costly for their old labor force from Corona to live around here or make the commute, so they have been replaced by Orange County locals who have to be paid a lot more. So their direct manufacturing labor and overhead costs, plus G&A must surely have gone up significantly," answered Max.

"You are correct," said Jay. "That shows clearly in the historic financial statements that Krantz sent us to review. But why would a guy running a company with declining sales and earnings *increase* his costs? He should have done the reverse – moved further out in Riverside County to get even cheaper labor and overhead. Right?"

"Yes Jay, absolutely. But the clue to the answer was there when we stepped into this lobby. Jerry Krantz just didn't like being in grimy Corona in Riverside County where he had to have lunch at the local Tio Taco stand – the Corona he likes is just a few miles down the coast, toney Corona del Mar with white table cloth restaurants overlooking the blue Pacific. In other words, his affinity for the good life takes precedence over good business judgment. Now regarding our mission, we are here this morning at the request of my friend Robert Patterson."

"Your big banker buddy? What's the connection?"

"He has banked CCI for years, starting with Harold Krantz, the founder and the father of Jerry."

"Don't tell me," said Jay, "the loan is in trouble and we are doing the bank a favor by nosing around and telling them what's going on, right? Is this another *pro bono* project for us? I thought you always stressed that we need to be paid for what we do," he added somewhat sarcastically.

"Listen, Jay," Max shot back rather sharply, "right now you

need to be thinking of this as an interview with a potential new *paying* client. Further, you should know the difference between *pro bono* and *quid pro quo*. I would not be where I am today if I did not make reasoned judgments about what I do for charities and what I do for business. I have a number of relationships with what one might call 'centers of influence.' I do things for them and they do things for me, and we know we can count on each other. Immediate payoff is not necessarily a consideration. Robert Patterson is one of those guys. This is *quid pro quo*. Are you okay with that?"

"Sorry, Boss. That's why you're the cerebral *Wise Man* and I'm just the cocky *Wise Guy* trying to learn at the master's feet."

"Fine, Jay, now let's move on," said Max, showing a broader smile than usual and continuing, "we haven't seen the rest of the facility yet, but I bet we will find that throughout there is a greater investment in office furniture, décor, and artwork than in production machinery. This place reminds me of Willow Industries."

"Never heard of them or it – who are they?"

"Willow is one of the classic examples of mismanagement and corporate excess, Enron but on a smaller scale. When they were still active 20 or 30 years ago it was a public company headquartered not too far from where we are today. Let me show you a couple of pictures that I've carried around with me for years."

Max retrieved two photographs from his briefcase and laid the first on the coffee table in front of Jay. It showed an impressive building standing behind an elaborate gate, surrounded by lush landscaping, fountains and rock walls.

"Looks like a Four Seasons resort or an exclusive Beverly

Hills country club," Jay commented.

"Exactly the correct first impression. But it is actually the corporate headquarters for Willow, right after they raised maybe $300 million in a public offering and maybe five years before they had to file for bankruptcy. If you had been inside, you would have seen very expensive furniture, art work, fish tanks, sculpture – you name it, very much like what we are looking at here this morning. The point is that all that money was lavished on executive surroundings, rather than invested in productive assets. Oh, and by the way, they also had a corporate Lear jet."

"But isn't a corporate jet a productive tool, like making it easier to visit remote facilities and customers and so forth?" Jay asked.

"That's the BS rationale you always hear. But the reality is you can almost always get anywhere you need to go faster, cheaper, and safer by flying commercially. And, if you must get a team to Outer Mongolia by tomorrow you can charter somebody else's jet. You could rent Air Force One by the hour for a fraction of the annual ownership, maintenance and crew costs of owning your own plane. Even NFL teams, the top dogs in professional sports, charter commercial jets to fly around the country. The players love it because the airlines use their sexiest flight attendants and somebody else cleans up after their food fights. No, Jay, the dirty little secret is that a corporate jet is really just a tangible expression of the CEO's sex organ, the ultimate phallic symbol and ego trip. Let me pass on a tip from those in the know on Wall Street: better sell short the stock of any company when the news breaks that they just bought their first jet, you'll make money after it tanks down the road. Enough of that, now take a look at this other picture."

The second photo was a shot of a modest office suite in a

rather rundown small industrial park. Weeds were growing along the edges of the parking spaces. The letters and numbers on the door of the suite were the kind you would buy for a couple of bucks at a hardware store and stick on the glass.

"Looks like a shady import/export outfit or down and out carpet wholesaler," said Jay, proud of his clever observation.

"Can you make out the name on the door in the photo?" asked Max.

"Not quite - looks like two words, with the first starting with the letter *P*, I think."

"It's Price Club. This was the original Price Club corporate headquarters in San Diego."

"Are you serious? The guy who started Costco started here?" asked Jay in amazement.

"Yes, Sol Price, and yes, this was the exact office in the low rent district from which he managed the expansion of the most successful merchandising concept since Sears, Woolworth, Macy's and Target combined," answered Max.

"Wow, I remember a case study in business school about him. He was involved with Walmart also, wasn't he?"

"Not directly, but Sam Walton is on record as saying that he 'borrowed' the key concept for giant warehouse stores directly from Sol Price. Price actually originally operated a chain of discount warehouse stores called FedMart, before opening the Price Club membership warehouse stores that eventually became today's powerhouse known as Costco. Sol's business model had three simple elements – keep overhead at an absolute minimum, buy quality merchandise right, and don't waste a dime on paid advertising. Give the consumer real value and they will knock your doors down. So, what's your take on all this Jay?"

"That the guy we are about to meet this morning is no Sol Price."

"Good morning, gentlemen. I'm Jerry Krantz. Robert Patterson has told me a lot of great things about you, Mr. Kupperman. Sorry about the delay, I just had to deal with an annoying employee issue that has been festering. The thing I hate worst about running a business."

Jay made a mental note that he was sure Max shared about Krantz: *The man is weak.*

"Thanks for relaying the comments from Robert, Mr. Krantz," said Max warmly. "But I think it would be smart if I don't start believing my own press releases."

Smiling as they went on a first name basis, the three started down the corridor to begin the tour.

"I guess you fellows know the history. My Dad started the business in the 60's. His expertise was in the design of computer peripherals and we grew rapidly as PC's started showing up in more and more homes. I've been running things since he retired a few years ago," said Jerry.

"What is the present operating picture?" asked Max. "You must know the kind of work we do and the reason Patterson wanted to set up this meeting."

"I'll get into that. Frankly, it's kind of depressing. Let me show you around first."

Avoidance of the unpleasant, thought Jay as he made another mental note.

First stop was Jerry's trophy room; rare wood paneling on the walls with a dozen or so mounted animal heads. At one end of the room was a huge sofa covered in zebra skin, on one side of the sofa was the lower section of an elephant leg sawed off and hollowed out to form an ashtray. A pair of huge ivory tusks stood mounted on the floor on other side. Across the room was a magnificent stuffed male lion, mouth agape, muscular shoulder raised, giant paw reaching out to bring down imaginary prey.

Proud, beaming, Jerry said, "I've done six African safaris, got world class trophies of the Big Eight. Looking to nail a polar bear and big horn sheep next and then I uh, I - what's the trouble, Max?"

"Jerry, I believe in being direct, maybe brutally frank, but not rude if I can help it. I have to tell you this display is very troubling in two ways. First, on a personal level I am offended by what this represents. I abhor killing, unless it is the execution of crooked executives and shooting failed companies to put them out of their misery. Second, to the point of our visit today, this represents a mindset that shows you are very much out of touch with both the world we are living in and the realities of the financial situation you and your company find yourself in."

"Well, I guess you are entitled to your opinion, but I think I ought to be able to spend my money any way I want," Jerry protested defensively, almost whining.

"That's what a spoiled rock star would say to justify shelling out mega-bucks for a full length coat made of fur from a rare snow leopard that had been killed illegally by a poacher. As far as it being your money, you know and we know it's really your father's money, isn't it?"

Jerry forced himself to pause before responding, remembering the recent stern warning from his father that the senior Krantz was going to stop making any more loans to cover the firm's negative cash flow; that he had advised the bank of that decision; that Patterson at the bank had told Jerry he better meet with Max right away and listen very carefully to what he had to say.

The three stood there awkwardly. Max relieved the tension by saying gently, as though reassuring a child, "Jerry, it is not our purpose to beat you up. I am a somewhat cynical, opinionated old curmudgeon, as Jay here can attest. You are not going to change my mind about certain things, nor I yours. But I know a thing or two about business problems and if we can help you, your family, and the bank in that regard, let's give it a try."

Relieved that a confrontation was avoided, Jerry said softly, "let's get out of this room and sit in my office for just a bit before continuing on, if we may."

Jerry spoke earnestly, in almost a stream of consciousness manner. He told of his upbringing, the way his father had spoiled him and his siblings.

"I was one of those kids who went bumming around Europe after graduation from prep school, instead of having to work at a summer job to earn money for college. At Stanford I hung with the same crowd. I realize now that Dad made the same mistake a lot of self-made men make, wanting their kids to have all the things they never had. I say I realize it, but I obviously haven't changed my behavior, have I? I was raised in the good life and I've always had what I guess you would say are uh, extravagant tastes."

"Jerry, being honest with yourself is always the first step and we appreciate your candor. Again, let's try now to focus on the business, agreed?" Max said, with an expression that indicated he well understood what Jerry was saying, that he'd heard it all before.

"You bet, Max. Sorry, I just had to get that off my chest. Thanks for listening."

Next stop down the hall was what Jerry said was the Information Technology and Engineering Department. Entering, Jerry introduced the visitors to Dennis and Brad. Dennis was almost a dead ringer for Willie Nelson, same headband, same ponytail, classic aging hippie. He wore a faded Hawaiian shirt, shorts and Birkenstock sandals. The visitors took in the scene and noted that Dennis had been occupying himself by tossing wadded paper balls into a wastepaper basket with a miniature basketball hoop mounted on it; the shots that missed were all over the floor.

Brad was grossly overweight, wearing the kind of size 4X polo shirt fat men wear in the hope that it will hide the fat, but instead always allows the rolls to show even more. He was riveted to a computer screen when the three walked in. Jay, with his observation powers and current computer knowledge, instantly recognized a game of *Warlocks and Witches* in progress on the screen. He glanced at Max and got a confirming nod.

The phone rang.

"That's fan-TAS-tic!" said Brad to the caller, then turning to Dennis said, "the guy from the barbeque place just delivered the ribs to the lobby out front. Let's go eat –I'm starved!"

As the two hustled out, Dennis tossed back to no one in particular, "uh - see you dudes later, it's lunch time. Hey, just make yourselves at home, be back around 2."

Max and Jay looked at their watches, then at each other. It was 11:10.

Jerry sagged into a chair at a long folding table and motioned to Max and Jay to sit also. Max pushed an old pizza box off to one side and said, "Jerry, the inmates are running the asylum. Your engineer is spending his time playing wastepaper basketball and your IT guy is engrossed in - what was that on the screen, Jay?"

"One of the hot fantasy internet games. People create mythical kingdoms, stay up all night playing against one another. Kind of the same crowd that go to the comic book conventions in weird outfits," Jay responded.

Wearily, Jerry replied, "I know, I know. Dennis was one of my Dad's original hires. He is supposed to be working on new product designs but I can't tell you how long it has been since we have brought out a promising new product. Brad moved here from Missouri at the suggestion of a guy in shipping who knew somebody who knew him. I have to confess we never checked him out. I guess we have done a lot of that over the years, hired the friend of a friend. Anyway, he *supposedly* is a pretty good computer whiz but I have the feeling his skills are dated, and as you can see all he is really interested in is feeding his face. Look, I know I should be more on top of these guys but I have always heard that creative people should be left along, to let their creative juices flow."

Jay could not resist the perfect rejoinder. "The only juices flowing are the ones in their stomachs digesting the last meal these guys pigged out on."

"So what do I do?" Jerry pleaded.

"Fire them both." said Max firmly.

"What? I - I couldn't do that! No way. Dennis has been here practically since day one. Brad is our IT guy. How would we manage?"

"Let's take Brad first, Jerry. Unless you are heavy into internet commerce or, like the big banks, have a critical need to maintain real time data transfer, Information Technology is not usually a core function, and in smaller organizations is a perfect candidate for outsourcing. You don't need somebody on staff just to make sure email gets delivered. Outfits and individuals who do this stuff are readily available by the hour, 24 hours a day, 7 days a week, backed up by using cloud computing. You could even put them on a small monthly retainer as an independent contractor and still be much better off than bearing the expense of a full time employee. Successful companies continually strive to make sure the *only functions they keep in house are those that relate directly to revenue production, the core functions.* The rest is overhead, and should be farmed out to the greatest extent possible, so you are only paying for what you need when you really need it," answered Max.

"As to Dennis, you have already told us the new product pipeline has dried up, so what is his contribution to the organization currently? In business you only get rewarded for what you are producing now, not when you joined the firm 35 years ago. This guy is a short timer with no tread left on his tires, or gas in his tank. He is just hanging on, drawing big bucks secure in the knowledge that he is untouchable because he was one of your father's pets. Am I right?"

"Well, I *could* fire him. After all, I *am* the President!"

Max smiled. "You sound like Richard Nixon trying to

convince the world that he had real authority just before he was forced to resign."

He went on forcefully. "Real power, and effective leadership comes only from perceived and actual competence, never from position or title. Let me repeat – *you must be competent to be a successful leader*. If your particular skills are heavy in one area and not another, you must surround yourself with key people possessing the strengths you don't have. And, it's not a popularity contest. If you are always worried about being liked, you're sunk and the organization is drifting, rudderless. Usually it's better to be feared than liked, and have the courage to even be *disliked*, as long as you possess and demonstrate true competence over the long run.

"Yes, you are the President, but a good look at how this place operates is all the evidence one needs to conclude that, while a lot of folks may superficially think you're a good guy, they don't have much respect for your executive and management skills. And the irony is, the more you waffle and try to be their buddy, the more they will secretly hate you for it. Dennis isn't the only untouchable around here. Of course, if we were to ask your employees, they would tell us what a great place this is to work – beautiful surroundings, nobody hassling you, long lunches, lots of breaks, coming and going when you please.

"This place is more like the Shady Side Rest Home for Weary Minds and Bodies than a real business. There is no drive, no sense of urgency. From the minute you walk in the front door, you pick up the atmosphere of waste, of misdirected investment. Your receptionist is the type you would have found working at Enron or on Wall Street in the go-go days. Get rid of her and instead have a sign-in sheet and bell that visitors can ring when they arrive, and get their own coffee from a machine. Replace the live plants with a few artificial ones from Walmart or Costco. Drain the aquarium and set the fish free. Send the couple who dust the leaves of the plants packing. These few changes alone should save maybe 150 grand a year. You know what I'm saying, Jerry."

"I thought you said you weren't here to beat me up," Jerry pleaded softly.

"We're not, but would you rather pay your psychiatrist money to give you warm fuzzies and tell you what you want to hear, or hit you between the eyes with the truth, with what you really *need* to hear? False reassurance is what a mother gives her kids; a dose of reality is the father's job, and *that's* why I'm here, my boy."

Another awkward pause followed, during which Jerry considered ending the conversation immediately and escorting the visitors out. He told himself that was one way to prove to these guys that he *did* have balls – he would fire Max!

But almost immediately that same inner voice from before intervened – his father telling him he had better listen and do something, that the gravy train was running out of steam and grinding to halt. He simply looked at Max and nodded yes.

"Jerry, before we came this morning Jay did a review of the financial data Patterson had asked you to send us. Jay has also looked at your history and product line and done some research on the industry. I am going to ask him to pick it up at this point."

Max was very proud of Jay, as he watched the young man begin a masterful analysis of the multiple challenges facing Computer Concepts, Inc.

Jay first cautioned Jerry that his review was preliminary. But his brief outline of the declining fortunes of the company was nevertheless spot on. They had been losing customers to cheaper imports; many of their utility and design patents had limited remaining lives. Their product offerings were becoming more like commodities, which meant that they would eventually face serious competition from those firms who were the low cost producers. And, to be a low cost producer you had to have economies of scale, low overhead and high productivity – three characteristics that were clearly missing at CCI.

As Jay was winding up his presentation, Max could tell from looking at Jerry that he was ready to throw in the towel.

"If I can't get all these slackers around here – and I guess I'm the Chief Slacker – to shape up, then maybe it is time to just close the doors," Jerry said, then adding, "of course as my Dad says, that is probably taking the easy way out."

"Look Jerry," said Max, "this is a company with a long history, that still has viable distribution channels and a good reputation. It's a company that still has patent protection on some important products, that still has a core customer following that buys those products. Why would you throw that away before seeing what could be done to build on those strengths and restore some real value to the company?"

"Yeah, sounds reasonable but I don't think – no, I *know* I don't have what it takes to turn things around," Jerry answered honestly.

"You're right, Jerry and there is another issue besides your skills set. You have been the Gary Good Guy around here for so long that no one will take you seriously if you do an about face. The company needs a new CEO." Max said firmly.

Jerry jumped on the idea so quickly that Max and Jay both realized that had been his secret desire for a long time.

"There are a couple of ways to approach this," said Max, "we could recruit a new CEO using an executive search firm. That process usually produces a list of well qualified candidates that then gets trimmed down to Mr. or Ms. Right. The problem will be luring this superstar away from another company, because the top performers are almost always currently employed. Given the uncertainty of our situation, we would undoubtedly have to commit to a pretty rich employment contract to get someone to come on board here."

"What's your other suggestion?" asked Jerry.

"We will be better off, I think, bringing in an interim CEO," said Max. "There is some very good talent out there who would rather take on a short term assignment than make a long term career commitment. I have a couple of excellent candidates in mind right now."

"You do? Can you get one in here right away? What do you think the right guy will cost us?" Jerry was fired up.

"Jerry, we are probably looking at $150K base salary, plus bonus and participation in the improvement of the Total Value of the Enterprise, or *TVE* as its called. But here's the irony – we can make immediate room for that level of compensation just by implementing expense reductions like the few I alluded to earlier."

"Max, I don't need to think about it any longer – let's get started, right NOW!" said Jerry, beaming like somebody on death row who just got a pardon.

As they were winding up their discussion with the details of moving forward on the interim CEO project, Jerry stressed that he really wanted Max to oversee things.

"I don't know how to put together compensation programs, things like TVA and so forth."

Jay immediately thought to himself: *Not TVA Jerry - that stands for Tennessee Valley Authority, like from the 1930's - Jeez, listen to Max and get it right - it's TVE!*

Jerry continued "I would like you and Jay to do all of that, plus find the guy of course. And, uh, .I guess the best way to put it is - hold my hand through it all."

"Sure, Jerry, it will be our pleasure to help in any way that we can. We will prepare a project management agreement with an appropriate retainer and have it on your desk for signature tomorrow morning," said Max, "and I will start talking to my candidates immediately."

Jerry escorted the two men to back to the lobby with a air suggesting an enormous weight had been lifted from his shoulders. Jay took a last look around and thought: *Boy I bet nobody will recognize this place once our new guy starts shaking things up.*

"Oh, one more thing, Jerry," Max said in mock seriousness, "go down the hall now and see if Dennis and Brad are back at their desks yet. If they are not, give 'em both a final warning and take away their keys to the lunchroom."

Laughing, the three men shook hands and said goodbye until their next meeting.

"Who are you thinking of for this assignment Boss?" asked Jay as he and Max walked toward their parked cars.

"First choice is Charles Stevens. He's been there, done that, as they say. Proven track record as a CEO with full P&L responsibility in consumer electronics. Has successfully pulled off turnarounds under difficult circumstances. He and I are in sync, which is so important since we are going to remain involved in this project. He's in his early fifties, so he still has the energy to roll up his sleeves and get the job done. Also, he loves this kind of challenge – thinks of himself as sort of a business soldier of fortune being parachuted behind enemy lines and taking no prisoners. And there is another thing about Chuck -" Max paused.

"What's that?"

"He is tough as nails but with a non-threatening personality, kind of like Robert Gates, the former Secretary of Defense. That's especially important in this case because the shock of transitioning from Jerry Krantz's namby-pamby personality to a real businessman is going be quite an adjustment for folks."

"Sounds good to me. I have heard you mention this guy before. So what do you want me to do next?" Jay asked.

"Just one immediate task. Get the engagement agreement drafted and executed by Jerry and pick up a check for the retainer. You know how fussy I am about getting paid on these assignments that aren't *pro bono* projects," Max said with a wry smile and a wink at Jay.

Jay smiled, winked back and said affectionately, "ok, Boss – excuse me, but who's being a wise guy now?"

4

Live To Fight Another Day

BERTHA GINGRICH WAS THE POLAR OPPOSITE OF THE MISS Perfect Teeth that Max and Jay had met at CCI. She was middle aged, quite overweight and on the frumpy side. She wore sturdy shoes and minimum make-up. Her hair was done up in the kind of bun style that librarians wore; a mound they could stick a pencil in. Indeed, when she tied her thinning hair together with an elastic band she looked something like a Hefty trash bag. Like many women without natural beauty, she had figured out a long time ago that if she couldn't make it on her looks, she would have to make it on her skills and work ethic.

That suited Max perfectly, who always valued substance over form. He and Bertha worked together very well, and had for the 25 years she had been his secretary and office manager.

He picked up the interoffice extension. "The mail was just delivered, Mr. K. There is a letter marked 'personal'. I will bring it right in and then go through the other items, if that is all right," said Bertha.

"Thank you, Mrs. G. Give me a moment to read the letter and then ask Jay to come to my office please."

He paused for a moment, reflecting on the curious custom found in so many Old World establishments of addressing co-workers as 'Mr.' or 'Mrs.', followed by just the first letter of their surname. He smiled to himself as he realized that protocol held true even if people had worked together for 50 years. He wondered if the custom still prevailed with the current generation, then put the thought aside as he opened the envelope.

It was postmarked Sarasota, Florida and had a return address that read *Southwind Marina and Yacht Sales*. Underneath the printing was written *The Babbitts, Slip 23*. He unfolded the letter, saw that it contained a few photographs, and had another thought that it was nice in this age of email and digital attachments to get a real letter that you could hold in your hands as you read it.

Dear Max –
It has been a while and we hope this finds you well and still able to take on rescue projects like me and Phyllis! I was going to say greetings from Paradise, but that might be a bit of a stretch. Anyway, to bring you up to date all the legal mess is behind us. Of course everything we had went to paying the Clarks, the lawyers, and settling with the other investors. As you had predicted, the fact that we were willing to use our last penny to make restitution meant the regulators went pretty easy on me. Unfortunately, I did receive a permanent sanction that prevents me from doing some of the things to earn a living that I had hoped to be able to. I talked to that big developer that you introduced me to, but found I could not even get a license to sell real estate in Florida, or I guess any other state. But it turns out that you don't need a license to sell boats, so that's what I am doing, more about that later.
We love it here. I had spent a lot of time in Southwest Florida as a kid and Phyllis and I had vacationed here from time to time. The Gulf of Mexico is beautiful, we think much prettier than coastal California and certainly a lot warmer!
When we moved here we first lived in one of those motels where you can rent rooms by the week or month. Phyllis got a job first, as a waitress at a place called Barnacle Bills. Can you believe it – this classy gal wearing a pirate

wench outfit and serving rum drinks and catch of the day dinners? Of course you can, because you knew her great qualities intuitively, knew what she was really all about.

Anyway, the restaurant is next door to this marina right on Sarasota Bay, and through Phyllis I got to know the guys doing the yacht sales and they hired me. You know me, always a good line of BS and I am doing pretty well selling boats instead of flaky investments. My boss says I remind him of the line 'the man wants a blue suit, so turn on the blue light'.

My first month I sold a $500,000 sport fisher and my commission was almost $30,000. We bought an old cabin cruiser that was at the marina and moved on board. If you know boats, you might know about these classics – a 57' Chris Craft Constellation. Beautiful lines and very roomy, the perfect live aboard. Constant maintenance though, as you would expect with a wooden hull over 50 years old.

But we love it! Most nights we sit out on the upper deck and enjoy our cocktails while watching the sunset, the pelicans and the parade of boats going up and down the Intercoastal Waterway, and listening to the tarpon splashing on the surface of the lagoon.

And we are living within our means for maybe the first time ever, and doing it TOGETHER, thanks to you my friend.

Come visit us here in Paradise when you can – this old tub has 3 full staterooms, much nicer than any pricey cruise ship!

All our best,

Phyllis and Len

PS – Say hello to Jay for us.

After Jay had finished reading the letter he started looking at the snapshots that Babbitt had sent along.

"Beautiful lines," he said.

"Yes, Jay – those old Chris Craft Constellations were the ultimate cruising yachts in their day and - what the heck are you smirking at?"

"Uh - you know me Boss, I wasn't talking about their boat, I am actually looking at this shot of Mrs. B in her skimpy pirate cocktail server get up at Barnacle Bills."

"Jay, I am only going to say this once more – stop it. What you think is funny and cute, I think is low class, crude and unprofessional. When you lapse into that mode it takes away from the great work you do, like on our CCI project. It also reflects poorly on me which I will not tolerate. Sure, you are the hotshot young buck and I am the stuffy straight laced old fossil with no sense of humor. But you know what? My name is on the sign, so I get to set the code of conduct. Understood?"

After a short pained silence Jay answered contritely, "understood." Then, drawing his hand across his mouth in the gesture of zipping his lips, added "shutting up."

"Good, thank you. Now let's take a break before our meeting with Dr. Arrowsmith, who is due in here at 10:30."

"Paul Arrowsmith, the molecular biologist? The fellow you met with a year or so ago? Would you like me to do anything to get ready for the meeting? Your wish is my command! *Zu befehl!*" Jay said, smiling, but completely without sarcasm.

"The same fellow Jay. I have not heard from him, nor has Robert Patterson since that long lunch when Robert spent so much time educating the man. Just take some notes when he gets here," Max answered, and thought to himself: *This is one of the things I really like about this kid, he doesn't sulk – I just called him out and he has bounced right back, ready to move on. A good trait, a very good trait. And I have to admire the little touch of humor . . . zu befehl, German for 'aye, aye sir'.*

Paul Arrowsmith looked haggard. He started off by telling Max and Jay he felt foolish and embarrassed because he had not followed any of the advice Patterson had given him, had gone ahead and partnered up with the wrong guy and was now in trouble.

"Is this the man you had mentioned to us at lunch?"

"Yes, the one who wanted me to buy into his company."

"Paul, we need to clear a couple of things before you continue," said Max somewhat icily, as Jay thought: *You are about to find out another truth about Maximilian Kupperman – he will go to the ends of the earth to help someone who is willing to follow his advice, but you will wind up on the wrong side of him if you blow him off.*

"First," continued Max, "I am no longer a practicing attorney so I can't give you legal advice per se. We can discuss business strategy, but if your situation dictates that you need a lawyer you must agree to retain counsel. If you wish we can recommend several good law firms. Second, I have to tell you I am disappointed to hear that you apparently didn't pay attention to what you learned from Mr. Patterson when we had lunch that day. That annoys me, because our mutual friend Gordon Jacobsen called me as a courtesy to you; I then set the lunch up with my friend Robert Patterson as a courtesy to Gordon; and Robert Patterson then responded as a courtesy to me. So in a sense you have let three people down by dropping the ball. That's not the way things work in business or personal relationships. Lastly, the meter on our fees started running when you came in here this morning. The combined rate for Mr. Rosen and myself is $750.00 an hour. If you wish to continue, Mrs. Gingrich will prepare a client agreement for you to execute acknowledging the above before we wind up our meeting."

"Max please," answered Paul sheepishly, "accept my apologies for my poor judgment and lack of follow through here. You are absolutely correct and there is no excuse for my lapse. Of course I will accept your conditions. I promise also to contact both Gordon and Robert Patterson and express my apology, regardless of what comes out of our meeting today."

"Fair enough, Paul. Just for my own edification, why *didn't* you get some outside advice before plunging in – from somebody, not me necessarily, but from *somebody*, as Robert urged you to?" asked Max.

"I intended to, and what Robert and you said really registered at the time. But when I suggested that to Brian – that's my partner – he said 'what do you want to do that for, these consultants, lawyers and so forth just charge you big bucks for advice you don't need'. Then Brian added, 'plus all those guys ever do is screw up a deal so much it never gets done'. Brian then told me he had other research scientists who wanted to hook up with him, and if I didn't want to do it, the opportunity would go to somebody else." Paul paused, adding, "I should have known right there that he had another agenda. Boy, I thought I was smarter than that."

"OK, Paul let's fast forward. What exactly is the situation now?" Max asked.

"Well, you recall that this fellow, Brian, wanted me to buy into his company on the basis that I would put up the working capital to develop certain products that he had in the pipeline, and we would be equal partners. In addition, I was supposed to be Chief Technology Officer and oversee R&D efforts going forward," answered Paul.

He continued, "I remember what you and Patterson said about making sure never to do business as an individual. Unfortunately, although Brian had originally set up a corporation, I found out later that it had been suspended in California for failure to pay franchise taxes."

"Was there a written agreement between the two of you?" asked Max.

"Yes, but Brain drafted it himself, telling me again, 'no need to waste money on those blood-sucking lawyers'."

Jay rolled his eyes and recalled another one of Max's sayings about using professionals: *You can pay me five grand now to do things right, or a hundred grand later to straighten out a mess.*

"Alright. Again Paul, what is the status of the business now?" Max persisted.

"Basically closed. Practically kaput. Just a few dollars trickling in but that won't last. There were so many issues right out of the gate. First, it turned out that two of the medical devices he had in development needed FDA 510k approvals, so that meant long expensive clinical trials before we could even hope to get proof of concept and *then* the approvals. Second, we were hit with a patent infringement lawsuit on the one device on the market that he did have some royalties from. Third, the bank we used was shut down by the FDIC."

"What is your personal exposure as a result of all this?"

"You mean beyond the almost $400,000 I put in?"

"That's a lot of money. Where did it come from?" asked Max, knowing he was not going to be happy with Paul's answer.

"That was the total of the 401K retirement accounts that my wife and I had. Basically all the money we had been able to put aside over the years."

"That was a huge mistake Paul. Your accountant has probably already told you that cashing in a 401k is a taxable event, although the loss on your investment could be offsetting. But the big thing is that segregated retirement accounts are normally beyond the reach of creditors. By dumping the money in the business you just dropped it in their laps. What about the bank?"

"Well, I just received a letter from the FDIC advising me that I was on the hook personally for the balance of the loan at the bank."

"What bank? And why were they shut down?" Max asked, now more curious.

"A little bank in Santa Monica. American Independent Merchants. What a joke, turns out they were actually based in the Cayman Islands. Rumor is that they were part of an international money laundering scheme, with funds going from Abu Dubai to the Caribbean, then on to Southern California. I guess they were under investigation by the regulators and FBI for some time. Have you heard about them?"

"I think I remember reading a piece by an investigative reporter for the Wall Street Journal recently," answered Max, then adding somewhat sarcastically, "I'm sure legitimate, respected bankers like Robert Patterson have the details. So you guaranteed the loan. Was the guarantee secured – specifically, did you give them a trust deed to any real estate?"

"Uh. . .yeah, I guess that would be the second mortgage on our home," Paul answered, voice dropping.

"That could be good or bad. Good, because there is something called the one-action rule, which means if the bank moves against the security and forecloses on the real estate, they can't then go after you for any deficiency. The laws have changed recently from state to state, and you are going to want to make sure about the current situation in California. But bottom line it is almost a certainty that you will lose your home in any case."

"Oh boy, I was hoping because the FDIC was involved they might just forget about me. You know, big government bureaucracy and all that."

"Wishful thinking Paul," said Max. "The FDIC has the power to liquidate assets of the bank to help pay off depositors. The loan portfolio represents the principle asset of the bank, and the FDIC has the ability and resources to pursue the borrowers on those loans to the ends of the earth. Indeed they have no choice, they have a mandate to take all reasonable steps to recover any taxpayer funds they advanced to cover depositors and creditors when they moved in and shut things down."

Max paused to let this sink in with Paul, then asked, "What about your other creditors?"

"Yeah, well since Brain flaked out on me I've been the one taking collection calls, like from the landlord looking for his rent and some suppliers we owe money to," Paul answered with a slight smile.

"Glad you can still smile, Paul. Usually creditor pressure is very difficult for even real tough guys to withstand."

"Well, the funny thing is, the nastiest calls are from this little local office supply outfit – not what I would have expected, they aren't owned that much. But the calls are very abusive, even threatening."

It was Max's turn to smile. "That's usually the way it is. You could owe millions to a big company but to them it's just business, not personal. But to the husband and wife who have a small janitorial service and who are owed $500 it's personal, not business. They will never forgive you for sticking it to them. Sometimes these small creditors are so emotional about it they can torpedo a sensible reorganization plan in a bankruptcy case."

"You mention bankruptcy – is that where I'm headed?"

"Yes, you, your wife and your partner as well," said Max

matter of factly. "And here is the main reason. When the corporation was suspended for unpaid franchise taxes, each of the owners lost the protection of the corporate shield and effectively became sole proprietors as far as creditors are concerned. That's easy for lawyers who sue you to discover, because the first thing they will do is check the status of the company with the Secretary of State. Of course, just to cover all bases, any lawsuit will name everyone – the company, you, your partner, fifty John Does, and maybe the guy driving the taxi cab past your office at the time you were ordering supplies. That's just the way it works. Moreover, if any of the creditors suspect that you or Brian might take off for Rio de Janeiro, they can get an immediate writ of attachment through what is known as an *ex parte hearing*. If they are successful your personal bank account can be attached the next day, without you even knowing what has happened.

"Remember, however, the decision to sue you is usually based on economics, not emotion and you might never hear from the outfits that are owed small amounts, except when they turn the account over to a collection agency. Bottom line – it's just smart to anticipate an ugly situation. That's why you want to prepare for a bankruptcy filing and at the same time hope you won't have to take that step. But a benefit is when creditors understand that you have done the planning, that fact alone is often sufficient to get them to back off and not sue."

"I guess I expected that would be the situation. But, there is another option I wanted to ask you about. My wife's mother has offered to refinance her home, scrape together other funds and loan me up to several hundred thousand, to help pay off these business debts. She says maybe it would also turn out to be a good investment, not just be helping my wife and me out of this mess."

"Paul, the short answer to that is – absolutely not. It is bad enough you have lost your own money, don't borrow your mother-in-law's and lose hers too. Amateur entrepreneurs often have what I call the *one more loan syndrome* – thinking all it takes is one more loan and all their problems are solved. This is a case of *sunk costs*. Do you know what is meant by that?"

"No, I don't," answered Paul.

"This is a hard concept for many people to understand. It is related to the old saying 'never put good money after bad'. Essentially, it means that it doesn't matter what you have already invested – that's gone, sunk. It only matters what the best use of the *new* money is. An example would be when small investors use the strategy of *dollar cost averaging*. Are you familiar with that?" Max asked.

"No, I don't think so. Is that . . . like a way to buy stock?"

"Yes, but not a strategy that savvy investors normally use. But it illustrates the point about sunk costs. Let's say you buy 100 shares of ABC Industries at $100 per share. It drops to $50 and you think: 'gee, I'll buy another 100 shares and lower my average cost to only $75 per share'. The fact that you already own the stock at the higher price is *completely irrelevant* to your decision about whether to buy more. The only question is whether an investment in ABC Industries makes sense at *whatever* price it is selling for at the time. Also, the momentum theory in the stock market says that once a company loses a percentage of value on the order of 50%, the price is likely headed even lower. So you could keep buying more and more and dollar average your position down to zero, equal to the value of the stock, effectively losing not only your original investment but new money on top of it."

Max saw Paul's rational scientist mind digesting the logic of what he just heard.

"I think I get it, Max. That means if my mother-in-law *did* have a chunk of money to invest, she should only turn it over to me if it was a better investment opportunity than anything else she might do."

"Exactly, Paul," Max said, pleased at Paul's grasp of the lesson. "Of course," he continued, "that analysis ignores the personal, emotional factor, like her desire to help both you and her daughter out of a jam. But that motivation should never be confused with a rational investment decision."

Paul was ready to move on. "Sounds like I need that referral to a good bankruptcy attorney like you mentioned earlier."

"Yes, Jay will work with you on that before you leave. And the names he gives you will be competent professionals who are both known *and* respected in our particular Federal Court District, which the Bankruptcy Court is part of. That local reputation and relationship with the judges is always important. Plus, these lawyers will all be well up on the most recent changes to the Bankruptcy Code, which is critical since Congress has made major changes to the code provisions at least twice since I was practicing.

"But first I want to go over the option of trying to salvage the business that you and your partner have. What we always do in these situations is figure out where the pressure is coming from, from which side of the balance sheet. If the asset side is in pretty good shape, that is cash flow from operations is healthy, but the liability side is a problem, that there is too much debt, or the wrong kind of debt – then we a have a company that can be salvaged, because you can always restructure debt as long as you're making money from operations. But as you said before, operations have essentially ceased, so there is no business left to turnaround.

Therefore the strategy is get you out on the best basis possible so that you can live to fight another day."

"I hear you, but right now I feel pretty discouraged and beat up."

"Of course you do," Max said gently. "But I urge you to put this in perspective. When you talk to Morris, or one of the other lawyers, you will find that bankruptcy is a powerful tool, so powerful you could stop a sheriff in his tracks in the very act of trying to seize your assets. As far as the stigma, in Silicon Valley it is almost a badge of distinction to have been involved with a failed company that went into bankruptcy. And remember, you might not even *have* to file, because the bank's collection options may be limited to the security as we talked about."

"But our house - our retirement nest egg . . . my wife, she . . . "

"She *what*? Are the two of you on the same page in facing this situation?" Max asked.

"Oh, for sure, for sure. In spite of my screw up in getting involved with Brian, Martha still believes in me, still trusts me, still says she knows we will get out of this mess." Paul smiled, then added, "there is something else about Martha. She always says that what a man does in life for a living is his whole identity, his very self worth. She reminds me that when a couple are at a social gathering, frequently the wife is asked 'tell me about your family' and the husband asked 'tell me what you do'. Understanding that a man always needs a good answer to that question, she has been a tremendous help to me all along the way, including working while I was getting my doctorate at MIT."

Max was listening reverently, an expression on his face almost like Pope John. Jay smiled, thinking: *Paul Arrowsmith you have done it. You won the old man over, you have touched his heart with one of his favorite themes – that of a clumsy fool who gets out of a jam with the help of a loyal and supportive wife. Good for you.*

Max was now almost beaming as he said, "then Paul, you are truly blessed. And you will get through this. It's time for you to do your own personal balance sheet, and I don't mean numbers. You have the bulk of your professional career ahead of you. Among your great assets are your education, your skills, your experience and your reputation, things that no one can ever take away from you. You will join a new firm and become a key part of a new research effort. And you know what? You will be more successful than before, be more effective than before, be a better team member than before – because you have tasted defeat and bounced back. You probably won't ever take an entrepreneurial flyer again, and that's alright – it's not for everyone. Because you now know what you should do and what you should not do, what you are good at, and maybe not so good at. You have found the very key to success – *make your strengths productive and your weaknesses irrelevant.*"

Max went on, "you will now be able to devote your considerable talents and efforts to finding that breakthrough drug or device that makes the world a better place. And this time around, your stock options with a new employer could pay off big. With Martha at your side you will do fine – and your mother-in-law can relax," he finished with a broad smile.

Grasping the old man's hand, Paul simply said, "thank you, Max. I feel as though I have a direction now, a course of action. Can you please tell me what I owe you? I want to pay you in full before leaving."

"Sure, Paul. However, I do want you to know that I actually

stopped the meter running on my services soon after you sat down earlier. So you are only going to be charged for the time Jay spends with you."

"Again, how can I thank you?" asked Paul.

"Just do two things. Make those calls and square things with Jacobsen and Patterson," Max answered.

"And most importantly – take care of that good wife of yours. She's your greatest asset."

5

Let's Make A Deal

CHARLES STEVENS WAS OBVIOUSLY PLEASED. AS HE GREETED Max and Jay, he said, "what has it been now – almost two full years? You know Max, I feel we have made some real progress here at CCI."

"We have been going over the financials all along, and the feedback I've gotten from Jerry, his father and Robert Patterson has been glowing, to say the least," said Max. "Good job Chuck, a very good job."

"Thanks, but really it was you delivering the wake-up calls that cleared the way for me to do what needed doing," answered Chuck graciously. "You know I have to laugh, here we are back in the low rent district in Corona, not too far from where they used to be in the old days. Jerry doesn't like the environment, but the move back here from Newport saved us almost $500K in overhead, not to mention big reductions in direct labor costs."

"And Jay and I we just noticed we had to get our own coffee

from the machine out front – no more window dressing receptionist," said Max, "another good move."

"That was just the first of many changes. You should have witnessed the drama and hand wringing when I said I was terminating Dennis. 'But . . . but . . . what if he sues us?' was the cry," Chuck paused. "I told 'em so what? First, I said, Dennis does not have an employment contract, and therefore in this state the *at will* doctrine governs. Second, and maybe more important, if we are *not* sued every once in a while it means we are carrying dead wood and not aggressively weeding out the poor performers like we should. We need to go on offense and set some examples from time to time."

"Boy, I could not agree more," responded Max. "One of the things I have observed over the years is that the firms with big productivity problems are often the ones where the HR folks are in charge, and they frustrate the efforts of managers to get rid of bad apples for fear of wrongful termination lawsuits. That kind of policy just produces more bad apples. By the way, *were* you sued by Dennis?"

"No, he made some rumbles but nothing came of it, as I expected. Last I heard he was happy just chilling and collecting unemployment. And I immediately hired a new young product development engineer, who has helped tremendously in upgrading our IP portfolio."

"What happened to Brad?" asked Jay.

"That guy had dated computer skills but at least he was smart enough to know he wouldn't survive long under the new regime, so he quit the same day I fired his buddy Dennis," Chuck smiled, adding, "I think he also suspected I would cancel his charge privileges at the pizza and rib joints and enroll him in weight watchers, which for him would be a fate worse than death."

The three laughed, as Max changed the subject. "You know Chuck, Jay has noted in his analysis that the balance sheet has really improved, with a healthy working capital ratio. It looks like liquidity has increased even faster than the increase in net income would suggest. Where did the cash come from?"

Chuck smiled again "I was able to convince Jerry to get Sotheby's to auction off virtually all the art, sculpture antiques and furnishings from the old office. That brought in almost a million bucks, a big chunk of which I immediately deployed in marketing and operations. We also have revenue from a whole new source, royalties from licensing a couple of our patents to outfits better suited to commercialize those particular products. We can talk more about that later."

"How about the animal trophies?" asked Jay.

Another smile from Chuck. "Jerry had a real hard time with all of that. I told him to sell the whole collection to Cabala or Abercrombie and Fitch if he didn't want to see it auctioned off; or better yet donate it all to the Smithsonian or Field Museum. In the end he put everything in storage. But not just *any* storage this facility had to be climate controlled, moth and mouse proof to keep the lion king's paw from being nibbled on."

The three men shared a brief laugh, and Max again steered the conversation back on track "We understand you have a proposal along the lines of selling the company."

"Yes, Max, and I want to get into that in depth as soon as Jerry gets here. When he arrives I would like you to first brief us in general on what's involved in selling a company, so that we can intelligently consider the alternatives."

"Chuck, before Jerry joins us – can you bring us up to speed on how you and he have gotten along, and his father as well?" asked Max.

"Sure. Let me take the senior Krantz first. I haven't had that much contact with him since I arrived, but I know from conversations with both Jerry and Robert Patterson that the older gentleman is very happy that he hasn't had to put any more money in the business. Plus, the exposure on his personal guarantee to the bank has been eliminated since we started making money and reducing debt.

"Regarding Jerry . . . you know Max, I remember you always said there were two categories of managers out there in the business world – the *competents* and the *incompetents*. And the incompetents could be divided into those who are *conscious* and those who are *unconscious*. Do I have it right?"

"Exactly, and it's gratifying to learn that you were listening closely. A lot of the time I feel folks tune me out because they don't like what they are hearing," Max said, smiling at Jay who smiled back.

Chuck laughed and responded, "well, I'll now prove to you I *was* listening – the *conscious incompetents* are dangerous, but the *unconscious incompetents* are not just dangerous but disastrous, because they don't know what they don't know – right?"

"I love it! When this assignment is over maybe you need to join Jay and myself in our efforts to change the world," answered Max.

"Maybe, we'll see. Right now I need to successfully conclude this mission," said Chuck seriously. "Anyway, as I am sure you had discovered, Jerry is a conscious incompetent – he *does* know his limitations and almost always gives in after just mild push back.

That has made my job of turning this place around easier. But there is an opportunity on the table now that we need to come to a mutual decision about."

As soon as Jerry joined the group Chuck went through a run down of events over the past couple of years. He managed to lay out the areas of improvement with a minimum of implied criticism of Jerry's prior management. He concluded with an outline of a proposal he had just received expressing an interest from a third party in buying the company.

"Henry Lee is the founder and CEO of this South Korean firm. A very sharp, capable entrepreneur," Chuck related. "As you guys probably know, the Taiwanese have dominated the computer peripherals business for years. But the Koreans have made real penetration in this area, just as they have in certain consumer electronics niches and automobiles. You guys are familiar I'm sure with Samsung, a good example of a very well run Korean firm putting out high quality products with innovative features. They actually are now one of the largest diversified conglomerates in the world. The Samsung Group is part of the Korean economic renaissance called the 'Miracle on the Han', which is the river running through Seoul, the capital. As a nation, and a culture these people are disciplined, hard-working and aggressive. Kind of like Japan a generation ago, but unlike Japan nowadays, South Korea is more competitive price-wise, and generally produces much higher quality than the rest of Asia."

"But aren't they the ones causing all the problems with developing the atomic bomb and stuff?" Jerry asked, as Max and Jay looked at each other trying to conceal their amazement at the question.

"Uh Jerry,. . .that's *North Korea* you're thinking of – totally different from *South Korea*, two separate countries. The two could not be more different, except in their shared ethnicity and early history. North Korea today is a closed totalitarian regime, pretty much totally isolated, while South Korea is a vibrant democracy, in the front ranks of developed nations and home to a number of successful firms," answered Chuck.

"Oh, sorry guys, I guess I uh, knew that," said Jerry with some embarrassment, as Jay thought to himself: *What planet are you on? You don't have to watch CNN all day long to know about the two Koreas. Jeez, I don't believe it. . .*

"Anyway, here's the deal," Chuck continued, "Mr. Lee needs a footprint, an established platform for distribution in the U.S. That's our strength. He is also interested in our intellectual property. You may know that we were able to make some product design improvements and refile on the core patents that still had good life remaining. That really increased the value of our IP portfolio. Our patent licensing agreements are icing on the cake, because that royalty income has only sunk cost associated with it and therefore is gravy for us. Lee values that as well."

"What's he going to pay?" asked Jerry excitedly.

"Uh . . . slow down a bit, if you would Jerry. I am getting to that. But first I wanted Max to outline for us the general process involved in a business sale or merger, so we know what the alternatives are. I don't have anywhere near his experience in that area."

Max took over. "Sure Chuck. The term commonly used is 'putting the company in play'. When a firm decides to do that, to put itself on the market, the traditional route is to retain what is known as a 'strategic advisor'. These are intermediaries, investment bankers. There are big ones, who arrange billion dollar transactions, and small boutique, regional or industry specialists who work with smaller companies. The effective minimum size of the client firm though, is about $30 million in annual sales, because the transaction costs are pretty much the same and it is just too expensive for them to take on a smaller company and try to sell it.

"By the way, I am not talking about the neighborhood business brokers here. They put individual buyers and sellers together for transactions involving mostly small businesses like beer bars, laundromats, retail stores and the like. There is a legitimate role for them, but to sell what I call a 'real business', you have to use an investment banker, or find a legitimate buyer somehow yourself."

"But," Jerry jumped in, "didn't we end the year with $30 million in sales, so wouldn't that be close enough to, you know, use one of those . . ."

Chuck cut him off firmly. "Yes, that was about our top line. But I think it's important to let Max finish walking us through the process, before getting into the actual numbers. OK Jerry?" Jay thought again to himself: *Wow, Jerry is already spending the money from a sale that hasn't even happened yet. The rent must be due on the trophy storage facility.*

"Let me try to wrap this up," Max continued. "Most investment bankers charge what is called a Lehman Formula Fee. In the old days it was a declining percentage of the sales price – 5% of the first million, 4% of the next million and so forth. In the last few years the formula has been doubled – 10% of the first million, 8% of the second, etc. In addition, they want fifty to a hundred thousand up front to put together the book."

"What do you mean a book? Book that says what?" Jerry asked naively.

"That's shorthand for a document that describes the subject company in great detail – background, markets, historic and projected financial statements, key personnel; in short everything a prospective buyer would want to know."

Jerry followed up with, "who publishes this book, who would buy it?"

"No, no," answered Max evenly, trying not to continue embarrassing Jerry. "It is not something that's published, nobody buys it. It is a document that the investment banker prepares and selectively distributes only to those potential buyers that have been carefully screened. The idea is to generate genuine interest in the firm that's for sale, and conduct a controlled auction where the only bidders are credible buyers. Frequently the investment banker has had a prior relationship with a potential buyer. That is, they have brought them other deals over a long period of time. The public never knows about these deals until an agreement is reached and an *LOI* is executed."

"Boy, more confusing terms. What does *that* one mean?"

"Sorry to be throwing more jargon out, Jerry but I'm almost done," said Max patiently. "LOI stands for *Letter of Intent*, and it is simply a summary of what the buyer and seller have agreed to; price, terms, conditions. Once that is signed, the buyer starts conducting what is known as *due diligence*, that is verifying that the information contained in the book is accurate and that there are no material misrepresentations about the company they are buying."

"OK, ok, but why don't we just sell to Lee and not fool with all of this?" Jerry asked, now sounding even more impatient.

Chuck jumped in. "What Max has described is the proper way for a business to maximize the payoff from a sale. In our case, we are fortunate to have connected with a credible potential buyer who found us without us going to the expense of hiring an intermediary to find him. That doesn't happen very often.

"But Jerry," he continued, "we – Max, Jay and myself – would not be doing our jobs if we didn't walk you through the process, so that you don't jump into this without understanding the alternatives. Otherwise it would be like hiring the first warm body that comes through the door, instead of evaluating a number of good candidates. That's the old 'friend of a friend' employment practice that you yourself have complained about in the past," he added dryly.

"Sorry, I keep interrupting like that," said Jerry. "I trust you guys to do the right thing. Let's continue, please."

"Right. I wanted to add another important thing about Henry Lee. He would be a *strategic* buyer, not a *financial* buyer."

"So what uh . . . could you tell me, uh . . . what's the difference?" Jerry asked timidly.

Chuck punted, "Max?"

"A financial buyer is just looking at the numbers and would just be making an investment to get a certain level of income. A strategic buyer typically is already in the industry, and looking for operating advantages by making the acquisition. They normally will pay more, because the company they're buying is *worth* more to them. In other words they would be a *premium* buyer, and that's good for us."

Chuck picked it back up. "I have had a couple of realistic discussions with Lee. He knows, and he knows I know, what transaction multiples are in this industry. He doesn't want to waste his time or ours. He has offered between five and seven times EBITDA, which is in the ballpark."

"Oh boy, more shorthand," groaned Jerry.

Chuck looked at Jay and gestured for the young man to jump in.

"Stands for *Earnings Before Interest Taxes Depreciation and Amortization*. Think of it simply as cash flow, as opposed to accounting profit and loss. It's the standard measure in buying and selling companies."

"Alright, ok," said Jerry, starting to fidget noticeably. "But what does that mean in dollars – what *are* we going to get for the company when all this is done?"

Chuck translated the EBITDA multiples into dollar amounts. "Our TTM cash flow – sorry Jerry, *TTM* stands for *trailing twelve months* – was just over $3 million, on the $27 million in sales, or 11%. That is actually better than what our similar size industry peers do. Using the five to seven times multiple, that make the sale price $15 to $21 million."

"Wow, $15 million would be plenty for me," Jerry said excitedly, "and since my Dad got his loans repaid and has other investments, he won't care what the number is."

"Jerry, slow down. Two things. First, we need to have a special shareholders' meeting to authorize the sale. That's when your father's wishes and desires will go on record. Second, right now we just have a range of value, a basis to negotiate a final price. Max, what do you say?"

"Correct on both points, Chuck. As we both know, you never want to jump too quickly at the buyer's first number. It suggests weakness or desperation, or both. In fact the buyer *expects* to negotiate, and is disappointed and even scared when you don't. If you set the tone for being too easy, when the buyer gets into their due diligence phase they will find a million reasons why the price should be adjusted even lower. Remember, when the LOI is executed you have set the maximum price to be paid and, at the same time granted to the buyer an exclusive right to buy the company at that price, or reduce the price, or just walk away from the deal if they discover something that they don't like."

"Absolutely," agreed Chuck. "Also, we want to try to negotiate a deal based for *future* results, not just last year's. If we're successful in doing that, it could make a multi-million dollar difference in the payoff, considering we have gained real traction in operations and the future, short term at least, looks pretty positive."

Jerry, after digesting the comments said thoughtfully, "well, alright . . . I will try to be patient while you fellows work through all this. After all, that's why I brought you three into this. Pretty smart move on my part, huh? So what happens next."

Max, Chuck and Jay all looked at each other and smiled at how Jerry was taking credit for the way things were turning out.

Max answered, "first thing Jerry, is to get shareholder approval to move forward. Your attorney, who is also corporate secretary could do this with consents following a telephonic meeting with you, your father, Chuck and myself all connected. Second, I would suggest Chuck be authorized to draft a response to Lee and map out a negotiating strategy, using the valuation multiples he just discussed. Agreed?"

"YES," Jerry almost shouted. "Let's get her done! Now, to celebrate, can I take you guys to dinner?"

Max said, "thanks for the invitation Jerry, but I know Chuck would agree that it's wise to wait to pop open the champagne until the deal is completed. And by completed, I mean not just the Purchase and Sale Agreement executed, but confirmation by the bank that the sale proceeds have been wire transferred to you and your father's accounts. Also, it's late and Jay and I have to get back to Irvine – we'll grab something to eat on our way. We will talk again in a day or so."

After they were seated at the Denny's right off the freeway, Jay opened the conversation.

"Well, Boss I would say this is going to turn out to be a very good outcome for the Krantz family."

"Yes, it will Jay. But. . ."

"But what? What's wrong Boss?"

"The family is very lucky. This could easily have turned out to be another example of the three generation rule."

"The what rule?"

"Three generations from shirtsleeves to shirtsleeves. I'm sure you have heard me mention that before – that's where the grandfather wheels a wheelbarrow and builds up a construction company with the sweat of his brow. Then the incompetent son blows it all and the grandson has to start off broke wheeling a wheelbarrow again. You see that so often in family businesses."

"Yeah, I remember, and now that you mention it - we *have* seen that a lot." said Jay. "Why do you think that is?"

"Not sure, but I suspect it has to do with second generation lack of drive, ambition. The 'life too easy' syndrome that Krantz himself alluded to. But it probably goes deeper than that - son never being able to measure up to successful father, feelings of inferiority, inadequacy or some such. But . . . I guess I . . . uh, will have to leave it to others to figure out someday."

"I think there is something else on your mind, Boss," Jay said quietly.

"I'm tired Jay. I've been at this a long time, saving people from themselves. I feel more and more as though I'm wandering aimlessly in a desert of incompetence, present company excepted of course," Max said, looking straight at Jay and continuing, "you know in this great democracy of ours with our passion for individual freedom, we have the ultimate freedom – the freedom to be stupid, to do stupid things. Look at the clients we have worked with over the last few years and the idiotic decisions many of them have made. It drives me nuts sometimes."

Jay was surprised to hear this tone from Max. He knew the old man had little patience for repetitive bad behavior, but this air of almost bitter resignation was something he had not seen before.

"But Boss, you are the one who always says we need to learn from our mistakes, not fear making them."

"I know Jay, and I believe that. Sorry, don't mind me, I just have had the feeling lately of – what's the term – being 'burned out' or . . . something."

Max stirred his coffee cup and looked out of the restaurant window. "You know, I have been having more and more flashbacks of images from the past, memories of my childhood. Of my father especially, and of Janet, of so many good years with Sarah of course. And a crazy thing is I can remember the phone number of the dorm at Brooklyn College from sixty years ago, but sometimes now have trouble remembering my current number. And my old energy level is way down, I seem to run out of gas quickly these days."

Trying to be comforting Jay said, "hey cut it out, you are still the sharpest guy on six continents."

"Thanks, but it's actually seven, including Antarctica." Then he returned to his earlier musings. "I had a wonderful English Literature teacher in high school, Miss Bowen. That's another great memory. Did your generation read Tennyson? God, I can close my eyes and see those lines from *Ulysses* so distinctly . . . "

> . . . *we are not now that strength which in old days*
> *moved earth and heaven; that which we are, we are* . . .

He saw the concern in Jay's face, and managed a little smile. But this was not the trademark smile that Jay had seen so often before. This smile told Jay that Max really wasn't his old self, that something else was going on.

Still trying to reassure Jay, the old man simply said, "that's enough of that. It's late. Let's go home now. Tomorrow's another day."

6

Sunrise, Sunset

JANET HAD BEEN WAITING IN THE SMALL ROOM ADJACENT TO the nurses' station only a short time.

"You are Mr. Kupperman's sister? I'm Dr. Cooper, his cardiologist. I understand you are the designated family member for medical emergencies."

"Yes Doctor, that's correct," Janet confirmed, anxiously. "What can you tell me? And please call me Janet."

"He is a very sick man. He has chronic congestive heart failure and his entire circulatory system is essentially breaking down. We have been unable to restore normal heart rhythm with electro-shock and drugs. Fluid is building now around his heart and lungs. He would be a candidate for a heart transplant except there are some age related risk factors, and there are other recipients ahead of him waiting for a donor. We are running out of time I'm afraid."

"So what is the prognosis?"

"He could experience fatal atrial fibrillation at any time. As you know he has given us a DNR order. If there is not an acute cardiac event, or perhaps a stroke, he will undergo progressive organ breakdown . . . " he paused, then continued somewhat mechanically, "and expire within the next few weeks."

"Does he know all this Doctor?" asked Janet.

Dr. Cooper smiled. "I'm sure you know your brother, Janet. He insists on being extremely candid and won't put up with anything less in others. Yes, he knows."

Janet smiled in return. "If you have been able to get to know him at all, you know he pushes hard to get at the truth and holds others to a pretty high standard." She looked off in the distance and smiled again. "He always loved to say 'I am wandering aimlessly in a desert of incompetence'."

Dr. Cooper laughed, "yes, I discovered that about him when I first saw him a year or so ago on Dr. Miller's recommendation. I know he is a remarkable man."

"A last question – is he in pain, is he comfortable?"

"Right now, pain no, comfortable yes. In between heart rhythm episodes he remains lucid – no, more than lucid – quite sharp. You can see he is pretty engaged in conversation with that young man who just entered his room. Is that his son?"

"No, that is Jay Rosen, his close business associate. My brother and sister-in-law never had children."

"Janet, I need to be continuing on my rounds now. Here's my card. Please call my cell phone if you have any questions or concerns. Dr. Miller or I will of course let you know immediately of any changes one way or the other."

"Thank you Doctor, for everything – especially your personal attention and concern. It is comforting to know he is getting this level of care."

"C'mon Jay, lighten up. One look at your face and you would think somebody's dying around here."

Trying to control himself Jay stammered, "sorry Boss, you know we wise guys can't handle emotional situations."

Max still had the strength to maintain some conversational give and take. "Yeah I know. Imagine how successful you would be if you were as tough and ornery as I am. Well, there is still hope – for you, not for me. Listen, we have work to do now.

"Get hold of our lawyer Barney immediately. Ask him to come to the hospital and bring the LLP organization documents and partnership agreement, this afternoon if possible."

Jay was close to the edge of the bed, tears in his eyes.

"Write this down and I will sign it before you leave. Ask the nursing supervisor to come in and witness my signature. That should satisfy Barney, just in case I am, you know . . . out of it when he gets here.

"Jay . . . before I continue, I just have to tell you what a tremendous job you have done for me from day one. And more than that . . . " Max was struggling now, had tears in his own eyes, " . . . you are like a son to me."

The two were holding hands tightly as Max regained some composure, "this memo means that from this day forward the firm is *Rosen & Company*. Congratulations, Jay – you are now the man."

Jay was crying openly. Max tried to relieve the emotion by saying, "you tell Mrs. G. that she better be as loyal and supportive to you as she has been to me, or I'll return from the grave and haunt her.

"One last thing – you can make all the wise cracks you want from now on, Jay. After all, it's now *your* name on the sign."

ABOUT THE AUTHOR

JIM REDMAN spent over 30 years living in California before semi-retiring to Arizona in 2004. During his professional career he served as CEO of a diversified industrial firm, and as CEO of a publicly traded company that did crisis management consulting for clients in various industries.

His formal legal assignments have included appointment as examiner with expanded powers, and receiver and trustee work on cases in the Federal District and California Superior Courts.

Since 1992 Jim has been the principal of Corporate Planning Resources, a consulting firm specializing in helping business owners and managers with transition issues. He has served on a number of corporate and community organization boards, and was a member of Young Presidents' Organization and Chairman of the San Diego Chapter of YPO.

Made in the USA
Lexington, KY
18 September 2016